MINUTE
GUIDE TO
MS-DOS® 6.2

Jennifer Fulton

alpha
books

A Division of Prentice Hall Computer Publishing

201 W. 103rd Street, Indianapolis, Indiana 46290 USA

GW00371726

I dedicate this book to my sister Pat, a great friend and a wonderful Maid of Honor. Thanks for all your help!

©1993 by Alpha Books

International Standard Book Number: 1-56761-416-7
Library of Congress Catalog Card Number: 93-73523

96 95 94 93   8 7 6 5 4 3 2 1

Interpretation of the printing code: the rightmost number of the first series of numbers is the year of the book's printing; the rightmost number of the second series of numbers is the number of the book's printing. For example, a printing code of 93-1 shows that the first printing of the book occurred in 1993.

Publisher: *Marie Butler-Knight*
Associate Publisher: *Lisa A. Bucki*
Managing Editor: *Elizabeth Keaffaber*
Development Editor: *Faithe Wempen*
Senior Production Editor: *Linda Hawkins*
Copy Editor: *Barry Childs-Helton*
Interior Design: *Amy Peppler-Adams*
Cover Design: *Dan Armstrong*
Indexer: *Jeanne Clark*
Production Team: *Gary Adair, Diana Bigham, Brad Chinn, Tim Cox, Meshell Dinn, Mark Enochs, Beth Rago, Marc Shector, Greg Sismic*

Special thanks to C. Herbert Feltner for ensuring the technical accuracy of this book.

Screen reproductions in this book were created by means of the program Collage Plus from Inner Media, Inc., Hollis, NH.

Printed in the United States of America

Contents

Introduction

DOS is something people forget about, until they are forced to use it. But when you need to use DOS to copy files or create directories, who wants to wade through thick manuals to find out how to do something that should have taken only a few minutes?

With your busy schedule, what you want is a simple, straightforward guide that teaches what you need to know, when you need to know it.

A few things are certain:

- You need a way to issue DOS commands without error.

- You need to learn the tasks necessary to accomplish your particular goals.

- You need a clear-cut, plain-English guide to learn about the basic features of MS-DOS.

  You need the *10 Minute Guide to MS-DOS 6.2*.

What Is the 10 Minute Guide?

The *10 Minute Guide* series is a new approach to learning to use computers. Because you don't have the time (or inclination) to teach yourself DOS by sifting through pages and pages of detailed information, the *10 Minute Guide* is designed to teach you the basic DOS skills you need to copy, delete, and undelete files, create and remove directories, and perform regular backups using MS-DOS 6.2—all this, and in lessons you can complete in ten minutes or less! And because each lesson is self-contained, you can go straight to the features you need to know about, starting and stopping whenever you like. You learn what you need to know, when you need to know it, progressing at your own pace.

Conventions Used in This Book

Each lesson is set up in an easy-to-use format. Steps that you must perform are numbered. Pictures of screens are included to show you what to expect. In addition, the following icons are used to mark definitions, warnings, and tips that help you understand what you're doing and tell you how to avoid trouble:

Plain English   This icon appears whenever a new term is defined.

Panic Button   This icon alerts you when you're likely to run into trouble.

Timesaver Tips   Tips offer shortcuts and hints for using MS-DOS 6.2 in the most effective way.

MS-DOS 6.0   This icon helps 6.0 users identify procedures that might be different for them.

In addition, the following conventions provide a clear idea of what to do:

What you type	Information you type appears in bold color type.
Press Enter	Keys you press (or selections you make with the mouse) appear in color type.
On-screen text	Messages that are displayed on-screen appear in bold type.

Using This Book

On the front inside cover of this book, you will find easy instructions for installing MS-DOS 6.2 on your system. The back inside cover features a guide to entering DOS commands.

This book contains 21 lessons, each covering a specific task for using MS-DOS 6.2. You should complete each of the lessons, in order, until you feel comfortable using MS-DOS. After Lesson 5, you may want to skip around and complete only those lessons you need for your work.

Because the DOS Shell is not included with MS-DOS 6.2, this book assumes that you will be entering commands at the DOS prompt. If you prefer to issue commands through the Shell, and you've upgraded from a prior version of DOS, see Appendix A for help. Appendix B contains a DOS command reference, and Appendix C lets you see quickly what's new with DOS 6.0 and 6.2.

Acknowledgments

I would like to thank all of the wonderful people at Alpha Books, who realize that ten minutes is just about all the time we have nowadays to learn anything—and they make it fun!

Trademarks

All terms mentioned in this book that are known to be trademarks or service marks are listed below. In addition, terms suspected of being trademarks or service marks have been appropriately capitalized. Alpha Books cannot attest to the accuracy of this information. Use of a term in this book should not be regarded as affecting the validity of any trademark or service mark.

MS-DOS is a registered trademark of Microsoft Corporation.

Lesson

A First Look at DOS

In this lesson, you will learn how to start your PC. You will also learn more about DOS and what it does.

Starting Your PC

Before you can start learning about DOS, you'll need to start your PC so you'll have a way to practice what you learn. The process of starting a computer is called *booting*. When your PC boots, the disk operating system (DOS) is copied (*loaded*) into memory. *Memory* is the working area of your PC, where the computer temporarily stores information it needs. You can load DOS in one of two ways:

- **From the hard disk.** This is the most common way to load DOS. To boot a PC in this manner, simply turn on the PC, and DOS is copied from the hard disk into memory.

- **From a diskette.** If your PC does not have a hard disk, you will need to place a special disk (called a *system disk*) in drive A. To boot a PC in this manner, insert the MS-DOS 6.2 Startup/Support Diskette or another system disk into drive A, turn the PC on, and DOS is copied from the diskette into memory.

Protect Your Investment   To protect your original installation diskettes from accidental damage (especially if you use them to start your computer every day), you should make copies of them. If you don't know how to make copies, refer to Lesson 11 for more information.

Booting   The process of starting your PC and loading (copying) the operating system (DOS) into memory.

Memory   The working area of your computer, where the computer stores files temporarily as it works on them.

Hard Disk   Located inside your PC, the hard disk stores your permanent information, such as programs, documents, and DOS. The hard disk is usually referred to as *drive C*.

Entering the Date and Time

Once your PC is started, it may ask you to verify the current date and time. (If your PC has an internal clock, as most do, you may not see these prompts.) Make sure your system uses the correct date and time, because that is how DOS keeps track of changes. If you see the prompt:

Current date is 01-01-80

Enter new date:

then enter the current date (after the colon) in one of three formats. For example:

02-20-93

02/20/93

02.20.93

If you see the prompt:

Current time is 00:00:01

Enter new time:

then enter the current time (after the colon). Use military time (a 24-hour clock). For example, to enter 2:12 p.m., type **14:12** and press Enter. You may also enter the seconds, as in **14:12:33**.

Try It, You'll Like It!　If you don't see the DATE and TIME prompts when you start your PC, you can still try these commands by simply typing DATE and/or TIME at the DOS prompt, and pressing Enter.

What Is DOS?

DOS is the *disk operating system*, and as such, DOS is responsible for the operation of your computer. For example, a program may tell DOS to read the contents of a file, and DOS takes care of the details. (You'll learn more about files in Lesson 2, but for now, you can visualize placing papers in a file folder.)

Why do you need to know DOS? DOS is the Captain of your computer, controlling what it does and when. When you need to do something with the computer, such as copying a file or formatting a diskette, you tell DOS and it gets done. Learning more about DOS puts you in better control of your PC, and allows you to perform your daily computing tasks with greater ease.

What Is AUTOEXEC.BAT?

The DOS 6.2 installation program creates a file called AUTOEXEC.BAT. AUTOEXEC.BAT is a special *batch* file that executes commands (automatically, one at a time) when you start your computer.

In addition to the commands placed in the AUTOEXEC.BAT by the DOS 6.2 installation program, you can add your own commands to be executed at startup. For example, if you wanted to, you could place a command in the AUTOEXEC.BAT to start some other program automatically for you. Moreover, you can press the F8 key when you start your PC, and select which commands you want executed, skipping over the commands you don't want to use right now. You'll learn more about the AUTOEXEC.BAT file in future lessons.

What Is CONFIG.SYS?

The CONFIG.SYS file is used to customize DOS. Certain system defaults, such as the number of files that can be opened at one time, must be changed in order for some programs to function properly on your PC. As with the AUTOEXEC.BAT file, the DOS 6.2 installation program creates the CONFIG.SYS file for you.

As it does with the AUTOEXEC.BAT, the DOS 6 installation program places certain commands in the CONFIG.SYS file. For example, if you chose to install the Anti-virus program during DOS 6.2 installation, commands are placed in the CONFIG.SYS to start the Anti-virus program when you boot your computer.

As with the AUTOEXEC.BAT file, you can select which commands are executed within the CONFIG.SYS at start-up. This enables you to fine-tune your PC for the programs you'll be using throughout each day. You'll learn more about the CONFIG.SYS file in future lessons.

Using the DOS Command Line Versus Using the DOS Shell

DOS provides two ways for you to give it instructions: the *DOS command line* and the *DOS Shell.* When you use the DOS command line, you enter a string of characters at the *DOS prompt.* The DOS prompt looks something like **C>** or **C:\>.**

To enter a DOS command, you type the command after the DOS prompt. For example, the command **MEM** tells DOS to report how much available memory it has. You enter the command after the greater-than sign (>), as shown in Figure 1.1.

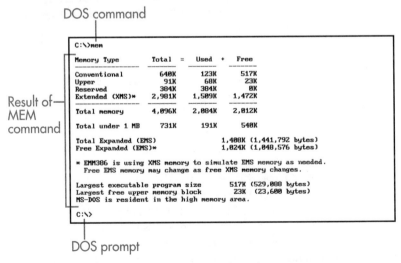

DOS command

Result of MEM command

```
C:\>mem

Memory Type        Total  =  Used  +   Free
----------------------------------------------
Conventional        640K      123K      517K
Upper                91K       68K       23K
Reserved            384K      384K        0K
Extended (XMS)*   2,981K    1,509K    1,472K
----------------------------------------------
Total memory      4,096K    2,084K    2,012K

Total under 1 MB    731K      191K      540K

Total Expanded (EMS)              1,408K (1,441,792 bytes)
Free Expanded (EMS)*              1,024K (1,048,576 bytes)

* EMM386 is using XMS memory to simulate EMS memory as needed.
  Free EMS memory may change as free XMS memory changes.

Largest executable program size    517K (529,088 bytes)
Largest free upper memory block     23K  (23,600 bytes)
MS-DOS is resident in the high memory area.

C:\>
```

DOS prompt

Figure 1.1 Entering commands at the DOS prompt.

After you type a DOS command, press the Enter key; DOS then performs the command. (When you press Enter after typing **MEM**, a report telling you how much memory your computer has available appears on the monitor.)

If you upgraded to DOS 6.2 from DOS 4, 5 or 6, you can issue commands not only from the command line, but from the DOS Shell. The DOS Shell, shown in Figure 1.2, is much easier for a new user to understand and to use than the command-line prompt.

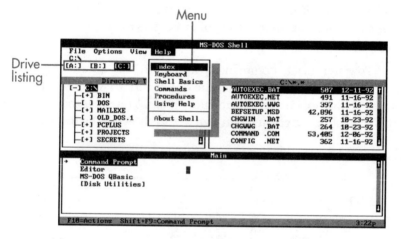

Figure 1.2 Using the DOS Shell to issue commands is easier.

Searching for the Shell by the Seashore? DOS 6.2 does not come with the DOS Shell program, but previous versions of DOS came with it, so it should still be on your computer if you upgraded from DOS 4, 5, or 6. If you want DOS Shell but don't have it, order the DOS 6.2 Supplemental Disk from Microsoft—see your documentation for details.

With the DOS Shell, you enter commands by selecting them from menus. A *menu* presents a list of choices for you to select from—with menus, you don't have to memorize command names in order to perform a DOS task.

> **Menu**   A menu is a list of possible tasks or commands. With a menu, the user doesn't memorize anything, but simply makes a choice from the options presented.

Some commands in the DOS Shell are issued by selecting a picture called an *icon*. If you want to use the DOS Shell to issue commands, refer to Appendix A for more help.

> **DOS Prompt, I Presume**   Because the DOS Shell does not come with DOS 6.2, this book assumes that you will be entering DOS commands at the DOS prompt.

In this lesson, you learned how to start your computer. You also learned about DOS and the role it plays. In the next lesson, you'll learn about disks, directories, and files.

Lesson

What Are Disks, Directories, and Files?

In this lesson, you will learn some basic computer terms: disks, directories, and files.

What Are Disks?

Your computer uses two types of disks: *hard disks* and *floppy disks*. Hard disks are for permanent storage of files and programs. Floppy disks (often called simply *diskettes*), are for portable (removable) storage.

Your computer's hard disk (usually drive C) is used to store your programs, documents, and DOS. You can copy these files onto diskettes, where they serve as backups in case the hard disk gets damaged in some way.

Diskettes are small plastic squares which are inserted into a slot in the front of your computer. Diskettes come in two sizes: 5 1/4 inches and 3 1/2 inches, as shown in Figure 2.1. Each size diskette comes in high-density and double-density versions. *Density* describes the amount of information the diskette can hold.

How can you tell what density a diskette is? Most diskettes are labeled, but if yours isn't, it's still pretty easy to tell: a 5 1/4-inch high-density diskette does not have a protection ring around its center hole, while a 5 1/4-inch double-density diskette does. Telling the difference between high- and double-density 3 1/2-inch diskettes is even easier: just look for two holes in opposite corners at one end of a high-density 3 1/2-inch diskette.

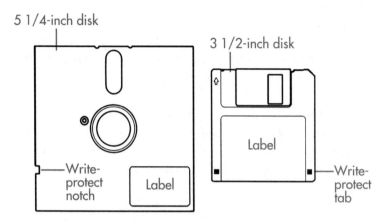

Figure 2.1 Diskettes come in two sizes.

Density The amount of information that a
diskette can hold. High-density diskettes hold at
least twice as much information as the same size
double-density diskettes, because the information
on high-density diskettes is packed closer together.

It's Your Density! Purchase diskettes that
match the type of diskette drive your computer
uses. This means you have to buy not only the
right size diskette (5 1/4-inch or 3 1/2-inch), *but
also the right density* (high-density or double-density).

Changing from One Disk Drive to Another

Disks are assigned letters. Your computer's first diskette
drive is called A, and a second diskette drive, if you have one,
is called B. Your computer's hard disk is called C, and additional hard disks are called D, E, and so on. A disk is represented by its drive letter, followed by a colon, as in C: and A:.

Changing from one drive to another enables you to access the files on that drive easily. To change to a particular drive, simply type the name of the drive you wish to change to, followed by a colon, as in:

B:

After typing this command, press Enter to tell DOS to execute it. This command changes you to drive B. To change back to drive C (the hard disk), type this:

C:

Make It Happen   Don't forget to press Enter!

What Are Files?

Hard disks and diskettes are used to store your data (*data* is a computer term for information). You save your data in files, like tiny books or file folders, each file named for the data it contains. You store different kinds of data in different files. For example, you might store a memo in one file, a picture of a boat in another file, and the fiscal budget in yet another file. Each file has its own name, just like a book, as shown in Figure 2.2.

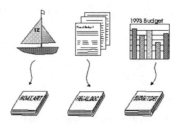

Figure 2.2   Files are like books, with their own names.

Filenames can have up to eight *characters* (letters or numbers). Most files names also have an *extension*, which helps to identify the contents or purpose of the file. For example, if you named a file **BUDGET.DOC**, the extension .DOC would identify the file as a document file. Some programs use special extensions to identify their own files. For example, Lotus 1-2-3 uses .WKS, WK1, WK3, or WK4 to identify its *worksheet* files.

Naming Your Files

The names of files must follow certain conventions:

- Filenames may contain up to eight *characters* plus an optional three-character extension. For example, **FISCAL94.WK3**, **YEAREND.DOC**, and **93TAXES.XLS**.

- A valid *character* is:

   Any letter, from A to Z.

   Any single-digit number, from 0 to 9.

   One of these special characters: **$ # & @ ! % ( ) - {** **} ' _ ` ^ ~**

- Uppercase is the same as lowercase. For example, the filename **WORK.DOC** is the same as **work.doc**.

- No spaces, commas, or backslashes (\) are allowed in filenames.

- Use a period only to separate the filename from the extension, as in **BUDGET.DOC**. You cannot include a period as part of the filename. For example, 93.MAR.DOC is *not a valid filename*.

What Are Directories?

With so many files, how does your computer keep track of
them? To use an analogy, book stores and libraries organize
books according to subject. In a similar manner, files on your
hard disk are typically organized by subject or purpose. For
example, the files for your word processing program are
kept in one place, while the files for your spreadsheet
program are kept in another.

In book stores and libraries, books are placed on
shelves. On disks, files are placed in *directories*. One special
directory is called the *root directory*. Think of the root
directory as the lobby of a building; just as rooms branch off
of a lobby, other directories branch off from the root. Only
general-purpose files (such as the CONFIG.SYS and
AUTOEXEC.BAT files) should be placed in the root directory.
The root directory is represented by a single backslash (\），
so the root directory of drive C is **C:**.

Branching out from the root directory, you create other
directories, one for each program you use. If you think of
these directories as rooms, you could have a room for word
processing, a room for spreadsheets, a room for drawing,
etc. These directories (or rooms) connect to the root directory (the lobby), as shown in Figure 2.3.

You can separate the files you create (documents) from
the program files by creating *subdirectories*. To continue our
room analogy, you could think of subdirectories as closets
within each room. Directories are represented by a
backslash, followed by the name of the directory, as in
C:\WORD. Subdirectories are separated from their parent
directory by another backslash, as in **C:\WORD\DOCS**. So
in this analogy, the C:\WORD directory contains the program
files that make your word processor work, and the
C:\WORD\DOCS contains the *files you create*.

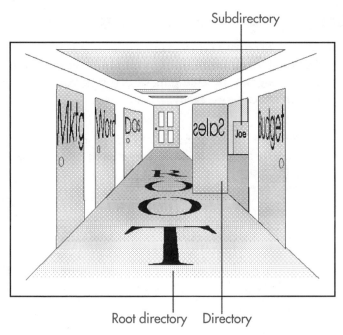

Figure 2.3 Organize your files in directories and subdirectories.

Congratulations—It's a Directory Directory names follow the exact same conventions as filenames, *although most users do not use an extension when naming a directory* (you can, if you want).

Keeping Organized The way you organize the files on your hard disk is up to you. Keeping your files organized makes it easier to locate them, and to make copies of them for safekeeping.

Changing From One Directory to Another

Because each *program* (application) you own is placed in its own directory, you change directories as you switch from program to program. By changing directories, you can access the program's files more easily.

Program   A set of instructions written in a special language that the PC understands. Typical programs include word processors, spreadsheets, databases, and games.

To change directories, use the CD command (CD stands for change **d**irectory). Simply type **CD** then a backslash (\\), followed by the name of the directory you want to go to. For example, to change to the DOS directory, type:

    CD\DOS

then press Enter. To change to a directory called WORD, use this command:

    CD\WORD

What Went Wrong?   Be careful to type a backslash (\\) and not a forward slash (/) when entering the CD command. Also, make sure to separate extra directory names with additional backslashes, as explained here.

Sometimes you'll create *subdirectories* (directories within other directories). For example, in your word processing directory (WORD) you might create a subdirectory called **PROJECTS** to store your own files. To change to the PROJECTS directory, you have to go through the WORD directory. (If you think back to the lobby/room analogy, changing to a *subdirectory* is like going through a bedroom to get to its closet.) To change to the PROJECTS directory, you would use the command:

CD\WORD\PROJECTS

Notice how an additional backslash (\) separates the directory names. To change to the root directory (the *lobby* of your computer as it were), type this:

CD

A backslash by itself means "root directory."

In this lesson, you learned what disks, files, and directories are. In the next lesson, you will learn how to enter DOS commands.

Lesson

Entering DOS Commands

In this lesson, you will learn how to enter DOS commands properly.

The DOS Prompt and What It Tells You

The DOS prompt is the on-screen marker that beckons you to enter a command. When you type a command, it appears after the prompt. The DOS prompt normally appears as:

C>

Since this type of prompt is not very informative, many people change the DOS prompt so that it shows the current drive and directory, as in:

C:\DOS>

Commands you type appear after your DOS prompt, as in (the command you type is shown here in color bold print):

C:\DOS>CD

Changing Your DOS Prompt

As you move from program to program, changing directories, it's easy to get lost and forget which directory you're in. Why should you care which directory you're in? Well, DOS commands act on files in the current directory—so for example, if you were deleting files, you could accidentally delete files in the *wrong directory* unless you knew which directory you were in. You can customize the DOS prompt so it displays the current directory, the current time, and other things. So instead of the rather boring and uninformative DOS prompt:

C>

You can change your DOS prompt into something really exciting, such as:

C:\DOS>

14:32 C:\DOS>

Tues 09-21-1993>

Promptness   Don't make the mistake that a lot of beginners do—which is typing the prompt, then the command. If you see a DOS command in a book (such as this one) which is displayed as:

C:\DOS>FORMAT A:

You should type only **FORMAT A:**. The rest is simply a prompt that you will see every time you press Enter.

There are lots of things that you can do with the DOS prompt to customize it to suit your needs. To change your DOS prompt, you use the PROMPT command. For example, to display the current drive and directory as shown in this prompt:

C:\WORD>

Type this:

PROMPT PG

Get Back!   To get back to the default DOS prompt, just type **PROMPT** and press Enter.

To display the date, include $D with the PROMPT command. To include the time, use $T. You can also include a message as part of the prompt. For example, to create this prompt:

The time is now 10:33 >

you type this command:

PROMPT The time is now $T $G

To get a two-line prompt, include $_ as in:

PROMPT The time is now T_PG

Which results in this prompt:

The time is now 10:33

C:\WORD>

But I Use Windows!   When you exit Windows temporarily to use DOS, it's easy to forget what you're doing. To remind yourself to type **EXIT** to return to Windows, customize the Windows/DOS prompt by including this command in your AUTOEXEC.BAT:

SET WINPMT=Type EXIT to return to Windows$_$P$G

As you can see, this command is similar to the PROMPT command. You'll learn how to add commands to your AUTOEXEC.BAT in Lesson 20.

How to Enter a DOS Command

Entering a DOS command is easy: just type the command, and press Enter. For example, for the current date, type DATE and press Enter. You can type DOS commands in upper- or lowercase. For example, the command **DATE** is the same as **date**. In this book, the command will look like this:

DATE

> **Entering the DOS Kingdom** Be sure to press Enter after each DOS command. Until you do, nothing will happen.

A DOS command is made up of three parts:

The command itself For example, the DIR command, which is used to list the files in a directory. (You'll learn more about DIR in Lesson 6.)

Applicable parameters *Parameters* tell DOS which files, directories, or drives with which to work. For example, you can type **DIR HARD2FND.DOC** to list a specific file with that name.

Applicable switches *Switches* are options you can use with a command. Switches are always preceded with a forward slash (/). For example, the DIR command has a switch (/P for "pause") that tells DIR to list enough files to fill a screen, then to pause until you're ready to see more files.

Between each part of a DOS command, you must insert a space (press the Spacebar). For example, the command:

DIR *.DOC /P

includes a single space after the *command* **DIR**, the *parameter* ***.DOC**, and the *command switch* **/P**. So although it may be hard to see the spaces in this book, always remember to type a space after each DOS command, and any other part of the command.

What to Do If You Make a Mistake

If you type a mistake *before you press Enter*, try one of these cures:

Press the Backspace key   Back up to erase the incorrect characters, and retype them.

Insert or delete characters   Use the arrow keys to move the blinking cursor to the place where you want to insert a character. Once you have the cursor positioned, press any character, and it will be inserted at that spot. To delete an extra character, press Delete or Del.

Press the Esc key   This will erase the entire line and let you start over. On most computers, when you press Esc, you will see a backslash (\), and the cursor will move down one line. Type your command there. (If you feel nervous about typing a command without the DOS prompt, press Enter after pressing Esc, and you'll be back to normal.)

If you've pressed Enter but got an error message because you mistyped the command, repeat the command by pressing F3. Then use the arrow keys to position the cursor where you'd like to insert or delete characters.

To stop a command in progress, hold down the Ctrl key while pressing the Break key. If you can't find the Break key, use Ctrl+C instead.

What's Up Doc? Pressing the Ctrl key with a letter or number produces the character ^ (caret). So if you press Ctrl+C, you will see **^C** on your monitor. Likewise, if you were to press Ctrl+D, you would see **^D**, and so on.

External Versus Internal Commands

One thing makes DOS commands a headache: some commands are *internal*—loaded into memory at startup (therefore ready to go)—and others are not. You can think of internal commands as being "built in."

When working with an *external* command, change to the DOS directory first. DOS won't know what the command is unless it can find it. (External DOS commands are stored in the DOS directory; if you change to that directory, DOS will recognize the command when you type it in.) A DOS external command is just like any other program or file—DOS can only find it if it's in the current directory. You could add a path in front of an external command, as in:

C:\DOS\FORMAT A:

But that's downright confusing. To give DOS access to *all the commands* (both internal and external)—*regardless* of what directory you're currently in—a permanent path must be created. To do this, the following command must be included in your AUTOEXEC.BAT file (the path to \DOS is added by the DOS 6.2 setup program. However, if someone has removed the PATH statement, you'll need to add it back in. Refer to Lesson 20 for instructions on how to edit your AUTOEXEC.BAT):

PATH=C:\DOS

The PATH command tells DOS to look for its external commands in the \DOS directory, so you don't have to worry about which directory you're in when you enter a command.

With this PATH statement in your AUTOEXEC.BAT, you could enter just this, and DOS would know what you mean:

FORMAT A:

> **Paths to Other Places**   You can include other directories in the PATH statement too, so that you can start your programs from any directory. (PATH finds only program files, not data files.) Just separate the directory names by semicolons. For example, my path looks like this: **PATH=C:\DOS;C:\WINDOWS;C:\WP51;C:\WORD.** As another tip, place the directories you use the most at the front of your path—since I use DOS and Windows the most, they are at the front of my path.

In this lesson, you learned what the DOS prompt is and how to customize it, how to enter a DOS command properly, and how to set up a permanent path to external DOS commands. In the next lesson, you'll learn some tricks for entering DOS commands hassle-free.

Lesson

Command Entry Tricks

In this lesson, you will learn additional information about entering DOS commands.

The Path to Success

In order to specify a file to be used with a command, you need to either change to the directory where the file is located (see Lesson 2) or include its complete path with the command.

Otherwise, DOS might get confused when it tries to locate the file you want the command to affect. The *path* for a file consists of its:

Drive   A drive designation is made up of the drive letter, followed by a colon (which indicates that you are talking about a disk drive). For example, if a file is located on drive C, then **C:** would be the first part of that file's path.

Directory path   A directory path is made up of a backslash (\) followed by the name of the directory, followed by another backslash. You can indicate a subdirectory by entering the name of the subdirectory, followed by another backslash. For example, if you had a file in a directory called DOCS, which is a subdirectory of WORD, the directory path would be **\WORD\DOCS**.

Filename   This part is easy—it's the name of the file, as in **BUDGET.DOC**.

The completed path would look like this:

C:\WORD\DOCS\BUDGET.DOC

You use a path to specify which file you want the DOS command to act upon (if that file is not in the current directory). For example, if you wanted to delete the BUDGET.DOC file, you'd use this command (you'll learn more about DEL in Lesson 8):

DEL C:\WORD\DOCS\BUDGET.DOC

> **Oh, My Tired Fingers!** Don't use the complete path for a filename unless you have to. If the file you are trying to use is located in the current directory, just type the filename, and DOS will know what you mean. For example, if you first changed to the \WORD\DOCS directory, you could type just **DEL BUDGET.DOC** to delete the budget file.

Using Wildcards to Specify Files in a Command

To specify a group of files to be used with a command, use *wildcards*. For example, you might type the command **DEL *.*** to delete all the files in the current directory (to specify files in another directory, use the file path as explained in the previous section). DOS provides two wildcards for specifying commands:

- The **asterisk (*)** represents several consecutive characters in a filename.

  For example, to specify all the files which end in **.DOC** (such as CHAMPION.DOC and FUNDRASR.DOC), type *.DOC.

To specify all the files that begin with BUDGET (such as BUDGET92.WKS, BUDGET93.WKS, and BUDGET93.CHT), type **BUDGET*.***.

To specify all the files in a directory, use *.*.

- The **question mark (?)** represents a single character within a filename.

  For example, to specify the files CHAP1.DOC through CHAP9.DOC (but not CHAP10.DOC), type **CHAP?.DOC**.

How to Interpret DOS Command Syntax

Some DOS commands have *parameters*, which tell DOS what file or other object to act upon. For example, the DEL command is used to delete a file. The parameter you use with the DEL command is the name of the file you want deleted, as in **DEL DUMBFILE**.

Some commands have additional options, called *switches*, that you enter after the command. For example, to see what programs are in memory, you enter **MEM /C**. Switches are entered with a forward slash (/). You can use as many switches as you want—for example, to display the programs in memory, one screenful at a time, you enter **MEM /C /P**.

To summarize—DOS commands consist of several elements:

The command itself   For example, **FORMAT**.

Optional parameters which explain what drives or files to act on   For example, **A:**.

Optional switches which allow a single command to act in a variety of ways   For example, **/F:360**.

The completed command could look like this:

FORMAT A: /F:360

This book lists DOS *command syntax* (a line which shows how to enter a command) using the following conventions:

What you type exactly as shown is capitalized. Even though it makes no difference whether you use upper- or lowercase letters when you enter DOS commands, they are usually displayed in all caps.

Things for which you must substitute a real name are shown in italics. For example, if a command requires you to enter the name of a file, it will be shown as *filename.ext*. Don't type the word **FILENAME.EXT**; instead, type the actual name of the file, such as **TAX93.WKS**.

Optional stuff is placed in square brackets. Square brackets [and] will surround a command's options. You don't need to use them unless they fit your situation.

Switches are displayed with a forward slash. For example, the page switch for the MEM command would be shown as [**/P**]. (Remember, the brackets indicate that the page switch is optional.)

A sample command syntax could look like this:

DEL [*d:*][*path*] *filename.ext*

The actual command you type—keeping in mind that brackets indicate options, and italics indicate where you substitute real information—could look like this:

DEL STUPID.DOC

or (following our sample command syntax):

DEL C:\WEIRD\STUPID.DOC

> **Syntactical Error?**   If you're having problems getting a command right, turn to Appendix B, which contains a DOS command syntax reference.

In this lesson, you learned how to specify a file path, how to specify a group of files for a command, and how to Interpret command syntax. In the next lesson, you'll learn how to access DOS Help.

Lesson

Getting Help

In this lesson, you will learn how to use the DOS Help system.

Quick Help for a Command

If you need help with the syntax of a command, you can refer to Appendix B, or you can get some help from DOS itself. Simply type the command followed by /? as in:

DIR /?

You'll see something like this:

Displays a list of files and subdirectories in a directory.

DIR [drive:][path][filename] [/P] [/W] [/A[[:]attribs]] [/O[[:]sortord]] [/S] [/B] [/L] [/C[H]]

Followed by a list of parameters and switches. For more detailed help, access the DOS Help system.

Accessing the DOS Help System

To access DOS Help, type the word HELP. Use the arrow keys to select a command, then press Enter. To go directly to a particular command, type it after the word **HELP**, as in:

HELP DIR

When you first access the DOS Help system, you see a listing of the syntax and the parameters for a command, as shown in Figure 5.1. Press Page Down to see more (press Page Up to go back).

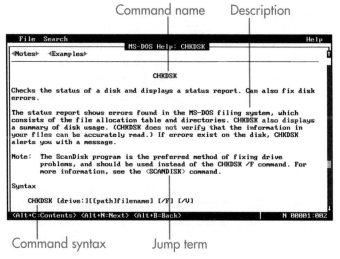

Figure 5.1   The DOS Help system.

If you see a word in angle brackets, such as **<Tree>**, it's a *jump term*. Press Tab until the cursor moves to a jump term, then press Enter to select it. You will move to another section of the Help system that contains information about the jump term. If you use a mouse, you can also *click* (press the left mouse button) on a jump term to select it.

> **Jump Term**   A highlighted term in the DOS Help system that, when selected, "jumps" to a related section of the Help system.

Moving Around

You can move alphabetically by command through the DOS Help system by pressing Alt+N for the next command, and Alt+B for the previous command. To access the table of contents, press Alt+C.

The Key to Success   To access menus and other items in the DOS Help system, you'll use *key combinations* such as **Alt+N**. In this example, simply press Alt and while holding it down, press N.

Quick Jump   You can jump forward, backward, or straight to the table of contents by clicking on Alt+N, Alt+B, or Alt+C at the bottom of any screen. If you want to use the keyboard, just press the indicated letters instead. For example, press the Alt and B keys together to move back one screen.

At the top of the first screen for each command, you will see the words **<Notes>** and **<Examples>**. Under **<Notes>**, you'll find additional tips and cautions about using the command. **<Examples>** lists several ways to type the command, as shown in Figure 5.2. Use the Tab key until the cursor moves to either of these items, and press Enter to select them. If you use a mouse, you can click on either <Notes> or <Examples> to select it.

To return to the syntax screen, select <Syntax>.

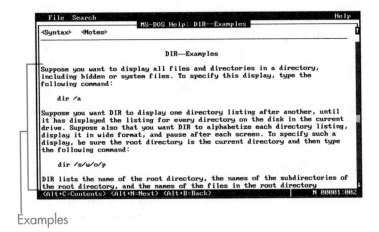

Examples

Figure 5.2   The DOS Help system includes examples for each command.

Searching for a Particular Command

Want to go to a particular command? Just follow these steps:

1. Open the Search menu by clicking on it or by pressing Alt+S.

2. Select Find by clicking on it or by pressing F.

3. Type the name of the command you're looking for, such as DIR.

4. Press Enter.

Printing the Help File

If you use particular commands quite often, you may want to print out parts of the DOS Help system for easy access. Printing part of DOS help is easy:

1. First, move to the section of the DOS Help system you wish to print.

2. Then open the File menu by pressing Alt+F or by clicking on it with the mouse.

3. With the menu open, select the Print command by pressing P or by clicking on it.

Exiting Help

To exit the Help system and return to a DOS prompt, press Alt+F to open the File menu. Press X to select Exit.

In this lesson, you learned how to get quick help for a command, and how to use the DOS Help system. In the next lesson, you'll learn how to list the files in a directory.

Lesson

Listing Files

In this lesson, you will learn how to list the files in a directory a variety of ways.

Listing the Files in a Directory

Using the DIR command to list the files in a directory is like reading the table of contents for a book—it's a great way to become familiar with your PC and find out what's on it. Or, if you've ever had the frustrating experience of misplacing a file that you were working on just moments ago, the DIR command can help you find it.

> **Comma Comment** If you have DOS 6.0, the directory listing you will see is similar to the one shown here in Figure 6.1. In DOS 6.2, however, commas were added to the listing to make large numbers easier to read.

The DIR command consists of three basic parts, two of which are optional (shown here in brackets):

DIR [*drive:\directory\filename*] [*/switches*]

You can type **DIR** alone, or follow it with a *filepath* (such as a drive or directory name), a *filename*, or optional switches. The complete syntax for the DIR command is listed in Appendix B. For now, let's start with the basics. To list the files in the current directory, type

DIR /P

and press Enter. You see something like Figure 6.1. The /P switch tells DOS to stop the file listing when it fills a screen. The figure shows a complete file listing, but if you see the message **Press any key to continue**, the entire file listing has not yet been displayed. To continue with the listing, just press Enter.

Whoa, Nellie!   You should always include the /P switch with the DIR command, to prevent file listings from running off your screen before you can read them. If you want, you can customize the DIR command so that it always includes /P. Add this command to your AUTOEXEC.BAT (see Lesson 20):

SET DIRCMD=/P

From then on, all you have to type is

DIR

and you'll really get **DIR /P**.

Wide Load   You can display files across the screen (instead of down) by including the **/W** parameter instead, as in **DIR /W**. However, the file information shown in Figure 6.1 will not be displayed.

DIR lists additional information about each file, besides its name. For example, the size of each file is listed in *bytes.*

Byte   The smallest unit of measurement of computer data, equal to one character, such as the letter J or the number 8. Larger data amounts are measured in *kilobytes* or *megabytes.*

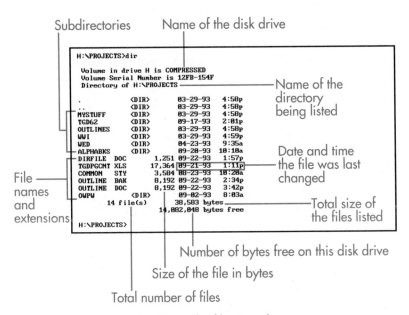

Subdirectories   Name of the disk drive

Name of the directory being listed

Date and time the file was last changed

File names and extensions

Total size of the files listed

Number of bytes free on this disk drive

Size of the file in bytes

Total number of files

Figure 6.1 Listing the files in a directory.

Kilobyte and Megabyte Roughly 1 thousand bytes (1,024 bytes) and 1 million bytes (1,048,576 bytes), respectively.

Listing the Files on Another Drive

When you're "talking" to DOS through the command prompt, it assumes that the current drive and directory is the "subject" of your conversation. That's why you get a listing of the files in the root directory of your hard disk when you type **DIR** at the **C:\>** prompt.

To list the files on another drive, you could change to that drive (as you learned in Lesson 2), then type DIR. But the simplest way to list files on another drive (such as a diskette) is to include the drive letter to list with the DIR command, as in:

DIR A:

Because you specified drive A, the files on drive A will be listed instead of those on C. This saves you the trouble of switching between drives.

Listing the Files in Another Directory

By default, DIR lists files in the *current directory* only. To see the contents of a different directory, you must either make the desired directory active by changing to that directory (as you learned in Lesson 2), then type DIR, or you must specify the directory name with the DIR command.

You can get dizzy changing directories all the time, so the easiest way to list files in another directory is to include the directory name with the DIR command. For example, if you wanted to list the files in the 123 directory without leaving the directory you're in, you would type:

DIR \123 /P

(Remember that the /P switch tells DIR to stop the listing at the bottom of a screen.) Even though you might be in, say, the WORD directory, the files in the 123 directory would be listed instead. It's like seeing into the next room without actually going into that room.

Listing Files in Alphabetical Order

Files normally are displayed in the order in which they are stored on disk, but you can force DOS to display the files in some kind of reasonable order, such as *alphabetically*. Type this:

DIR /O /P

This command lists subdirectories first, then files, sorted by file name. You can sort files in other ways; see DOS Help for more information.

Listing Selected Files

If you're looking for a particular file, or a particular file type (extension), you can use *wildcards* to list selected files. You learned about wildcards in Lesson 4, but as a quick review:

The asterisk (*) represents several characters within a file name. For example, ***.DOC** means "use files that have any first name, but a last name of DOC." Using **K*.DOC** means "use files that begin with K, followed by a bunch of miscellaneous characters, that have a last name of DOC. Using *.* means "use files with any first or last name"; in other words, "use all the files." Any characters after an asterisk are ignored, so **M*RCH.*** is the same as **M*.***.

The question mark (?) is used to represent a single character within a file name. For example, **JO?N.WKS** means "use files that begin with the letters JO, followed by any character, followed by an N, and the extension .WKS. The files JOHN.WKS and JOAN.WKS match this pattern, but the files JEAN.WKS and JOHNNY.WKS do not. You can use additional question marks to represent other characters, as in **JO??.WKS**, but the number of characters must also match. The files JOHN.WKS, JOKE.WKS and JOAN.WKS would match this file name pattern, but JOKES.WKS would not.

To list selected files, simply type DIR followed by the filename pattern, as in

DIR TAXES??.* /P

This command lists (one screenful at a time) all the files in the current directory that start with the letters TAXES, followed by two characters, and any extension.

Locating a File Across Several Directories

If you've ever had the experience of saving a file, only to lose it when you need to use it again, this variation of the DIR command will come in handy. You can use this command to locate a file anywhere on your hard disk. For example, to find the file LOST.DOC, you would type:

DIR C:\LOST.DOC /S

The /S switch tells DIR to look in the current directory, and all subdirectories. By adding C:\ in front of the filename, you told DIR to start its search not in the current directory, but in the root directory.

You can use wildcards to conduct more extensive searches. For example, if you wanted to list all the .DOC files on your hard disk, you would type:

DIR C:*.DOC /S /P

Printing a File Listing

When you use the DIR command (or any other command, for that matter), the result of that command is displayed on the monitor. You can *redirect* the output to a different device, such as your printer. Why do this? Sometimes it's easier to flip pages than to scan through a directory listing on screen. Also, a printout of their contents makes a great way to organize diskettes. To send a listing of all the files on a diskette in drive A to the printer, use this command:

DIR A: /W >PRN

The greater-than sign (>) is the *redirection symbol*; PRN is DOS's name for your printer. Since I want to print only the file names (and not the other DIR information), I included the /W switch.

Going Down?   If you want, you can print a plain file listing with the name of each file and nothing else. Use this command:

DIR A: /B > PRN

You can also send the file listing to another file, so you can save it permanently or print it out later. To save a listing of the current directory in a file, use a command like this:

DIR >FILE.LST

In this lesson, you learned how to list files in any directory, or on any drive. You also learned how to sort and/or print the file listing. In the next lesson, you'll learn how to copy and move files.

Lesson

Copying and Moving Files

In this lesson, you will learn how to copy or move files.

A Word Before You Copy or Move Files

When you copy a file, you end up with two files—the copy and the original. When you move a file, you still have only one file—it's just been moved to a different directory on your disk. When would you want to copy or move files? With the COPY command, you could easily make copies of important files and store them on diskettes for safekeeping. Should something happen to your PC's hard disk, you'd still have your original files (the programs you could reload from their original diskettes).

If you wanted to print a document on another PC, you could use the COPY command to place a copy of the document on diskette, and then you could use the COPY command again to copy the document from that diskette to the other PC's hard disk (or you could just print it from the diskette).

The MOVE command allows you to reorganize your documents so you can find them easily. Halfway through a project, for example, you could decide to create a subdirectory for all the files related to it. After creating the subdirectory (which you'll learn how to do in Lesson 9), you could move the files from their current directory to their private one.

Copying a File

The COPY command consists of three basic parts (remember to insert a space between each part of a command):

COPY *file(s)* [*destination*]

> **Which Way Did They Go?** You don't have to specify where to copy the files, but if you don't, DOS will copy them to the current directory or drive.

> **Don't Be Such a Copy Cat!** If you attempt to copy a file that will overwrite an existing copy of the same file, previous versions of DOS, including DOS 6.0, will let you do it. However, DOS 6.2 will let you know about the attempt to overwrite a file by prompting you. For example, if you copy the file BUDGET.WKS from a diskette into your \123 directory and a BUDGET.WKS file already exists there, you'll be prompted. Press Y to overwrite the file, or N to abort the copy process.

For example, suppose you wanted to copy your budget file onto a diskette in drive A for safekeeping. Type:

COPY BUDGET.WKS A:

and press Enter. If you get the message **File not found**, DOS was unable to find the BUDGET.WKS file. You could have misspelled the filename, but a likelier error is that you are not in the directory where the file is kept. In that case, change to the directory where the file is located, then type the COPY command again:

CD\123

COPY BUDGET.WKS A:

Or, if you prefer a one-step operation, include the file path with the COPY command (see Lesson 4 for a review on using file paths):

COPY C:\123\BUDGET.WKS A:

By the way, notice how there are only *two spaces* in the COPY command: one is placed after the word **COPY**, and the other is placed after the name of the file to copy.

Specifying the Name of the Copied File

You can make a copy of a file and place it in the same directory, but under a different name. This allows you to work on the copy, while the original file remains unchanged. For example, if you wanted to edit your AUTOEXEC.BAT (which you'll learn how to do in Lesson 20), I recommend making a copy of it first:

COPY AUTOEXEC.BAT AUTOEXEC.BKP

If you try this and you get **File not found**, change to the root directory (where the AUTOEXEC.BAT file is kept) and try again:

CD\

COPY AUTOEXEC.BAT AUTOEXEC.BKP

Remember to press Enter after each command. Because you did not include a drive or directory to which to copy the file (as you might have in **COPY AUTOEXEC.BAT C:\MYBACKUPS\AUTOEXEC.BKP**), the AUTOEXEC.BKP file is placed in the current directory (in this case, the root directory).

Renaming a File Instead of Copying It

If you just want to change the name of a file (and not make a copy, as we did with the AUTOEXEC.BAT file), use the REN command. The format of the REN (rename) command is simple:

REN *originalname newname*

For example, to rename your budget file to reflect the current year, type:

REN BUDGET.WKS BUDGET93.WKS

When renaming files, remember these things:

* Filenames can contain only *eight* characters.

* Don't change the extension of the file unless you know exactly what you're doing. (In our example, we kept the .WKS extension the same on the renamed file). Programs use these extensions to identify their files and their purpose, and if files are not named correctly, your program may not be able to use them.

Copying Several Files at Once

You can use DOS *wildcards* to specify more than one file to copy. As you learned in lesson 4, wildcards create a general filename pattern, so that several files can be used with a single DOS command. There are two DOS wildcards, the asterisk (*) and the question mark (?). The asterisk * represents several characters within a file name (as in *.**WKS**), and the question mark ? represents a single character within a file name (as in **CHAP??.DOC**). See Lesson 4 for a complete refresher on using wildcards.

For example, suppose you wanted to copy all the files in your \WORD directory ending in .DOC onto a diskette. Use these two commands:

CD\WORD

COPY *.DOC A:

Those Flying Fingers If you want to copy the files in one step, without changing to the \WORD directory, include the full pathname:

COPY C:\WORD*.DOC A:

Even though you save a step, it's a lot more typing. Choose whichever method is easier for you.

You can also use wildcards when duplicating files with the COPY command. For example, to create a duplicate of all the .WK1 files in the \SPREADST directory. Follow these steps:

CD\SPREADST

COPY *.WK1 *.BKP

This command creates a copy of all the files in the current directory with an extension of .WK1, and changes the extension on the copies to .BKP. Use wildcards in place of file names in any COPY command to copy multiple files at once.

Variations on the COPY Command

The COPY command is very versatile; you can use it to copy files from one directory to another, from your hard disk to a diskette, or from a diskette to your hard disk. Unfortunately, its versatility is what also makes the COPY command a bit difficult.

In this section, you'll find samples of common COPY situations. Use them as guides whenever you use the COPY command.

Copying Files to a Different Directory

Suppose you wanted to copy all your letters from the \WORD directory to a new directory called \LETTERS. (This will create copies of the files in two places; if you want to move files, see the last section in this lesson.) Type these commands:

CD\WORD

COPY *.LTR C:\LETTERS

To accomplish this in one step, use this command instead:

COPY C:\WORD*.LTR C:\LETTERS

Copying Files from a Directory to a Diskette

Suppose you needed to print one of your spreadsheets on a printer that is attached to another PC. To do this, you want to copy your spreadsheet file, YEAREND.WK1, from the \SPREADST directory to a diskette, then copy the file from that diskette to the other PC. Here are the two commands to accomplish the first part of this task:

CD\SPREADST

COPY YEAREND.WK1 A:

To accomplish this in one step, use this command instead:

COPY C:\SPREADST\YEAREND.WK1 A:

Copying Files from a Diskette to a Directory

Continuing our scenario, suppose you wanted to copy your spreadsheet file from your diskette to a directory called \123 on the PC with the printer. Enter these commands to change to the diskette drive that holds the file, and copy the file:

    A:

    COPY YEAREND.WK1 C:\123

    To accomplish this in one step, use this command instead:

    COPY A:\YEAREND.WK1 C:\123

Copying Files from One Diskette to Another

If your PC has two diskette drives, you can copy files from one diskette to another. Suppose you have a file called SALES.DOC on a diskette in drive A, and you want to copy that file to a diskette in drive B so you can use that file on a different PC. Start by changing to drive A, then copy the file to drive B:

    A:

    COPY SALES.DOC B:

    To accomplish this in one step, use this command instead:

    COPY A:\SALES.DOC B:

Moving Files

Moving files from one directory to another is simple with DOS 6.2. In an earlier example, you copied files from the \WORD directory to the \LETTERS directory. With the COPY command, the files resided in two places on your hard disk.

To move them instead, you use the MOVE command. The syntax for the MOVE command is similar to that of the COPY command:

MOVE *file(s)* [*destination*]

> **Copy Cat!** Like COPY, you don't have to specify where to move the files, but if you don't, DOS will move them to the current directory or drive. Also like COPY, there are only *two spaces* in this command—one space after **MOVE**, and another after the name of the file to move.

> **Bad Command?** If you get the error message **Bad command or filename** while using the MOVE command, you need to create a path to the \DOS directory. See Lesson 4.

To move those letters from the \WORD directory to the \LETTERS directory, type these commands:

CD\WORD

MOVE *.LTR C:\LETTERS

> **Don't Move Too Fast!** If you attempt to move a file, and it will overwrite an existing copy of the same file, previous versions of DOS, including DOS 6.0, will let you do it. However, DOS 6.2 will warn you by prompting you. For example, if you move the file BUDGET.WKS from your \PROJECTS into your \123 directory and a BUDGET.WKS file already exists there, you'll be prompted. Press Y to overwrite the file, or N to abort the move process.

You can include the file path with the MOVE command to perform the move in one step:

MOVE C:\WORD*.LTR C:\LETTERS

Get a Move On!   You can also rename a directory (in a sense, move the entire thing) with the MOVE command. See Lesson 9.

In this lesson, you learned how to copy and move files in a variety of ways. In the next lesson, you'll learn how to delete unwanted files (and how to get them back if you delete them accidentally).

Lesson

8

Deleting Files and Getting Them Back

In this lesson, you will learn how to delete files. Also, if you've accidently deleted a file, you will learn how to restore it.

Deleting a File

You will find yourself deleting files for many reasons: the files are outdated and you no longer use them, or you need to make room on your hard drive.

> **Making Room** If you are trying to relieve a congested hard drive, use the techniques described in Lesson 15 to back up selected files. Then follow the instructions in this lesson to delete the backed-up files. If you ever need the files again, you can restore them to your hard disk from your backup diskettes.
>
> Also, if space is a problem, you will want to use DoubleSpace to increase the amount of files your hard disk can hold. See Lesson 12 for more information.

> **Deleting Directories** If you want to delete an entire directory, refer to the instructions in Lesson 9.

To delete a file, you use the DEL command. The syntax for the DEL command is simple:

DEL *filename*

For example, suppose you wanted to delete a file called 92PROD.CHT, located in the \CHART directory. Use these commands:

CD\CHART

DEL 92PROD.CHT

Although you can usually retrieve a file deleted by accident, you should still be careful. That's why you might want to follow the two-step process shown here, instead of trying to perform a deletion in one step, as in:

DEL C:\CHART\92PROD.CHT

> **You Can't Do That!**   If you get the error message **Access denied** when using the DEL command, it means that the file is protected. Although there is a way to delete such a file (by using the ATTRIB command), it's usually not a good idea, since the file was protected for a reason. Consult a technical expert before proceeding.

Deleting Selected Files

Use DOS *wildcards* to delete selected files in a directory. DOS has two wildcards, the asterisk (which represents several characters within a file name, as in *.DOC) and the question mark (which represents a single character within a filename, as in **PART??.DOC**).

For example, suppose you wanted to delete all your 1993 files from the SALES directory. Follow these steps:

CD\SALES

DEL 93*.*

If a wildcard pattern fits most of the file you want, you can request confirmation for each file before it is deleted. Just add a /P switch (for prompt) at the end of the DEL command:

CD\SALES

DEL 93*.* /P

> **Pass the P's** If you remember from Lesson 6 that with the DIR command, the /P switch stood for "pause"—don't panic. Here it stands for "prompt."

DOS will prompt you before it deletes each file. Press Y to delete a file, or N to skip a file and not delete it.

> **Oops!** When using wildcards to delete files, use the **DIR** command first, to verify that you will delete the correct files. For example, to delete all the files in the current directory that begin with an M and use a .XLS extension, use this command first:
>
> DIR M*.XLS
>
> You'll see a listing of all the .XLS files in the current directory that begin with M. If you're satisfied that the listing contains all the files you want to delete, use the DEL command with the same wildcards:
>
> DEL M*.XLS

Deleting All the Files in a Directory

You can also use wildcards to delete all the files in a directory. Let's say that you had a directory called MONTHLY where you stored all the monthly departmental reports. Now that the month's over, and you want to remove all the files, but keep the directory.

To delete all the files in the \MONTHLY directory, use this command:

DEL C:\MONTHLY

Press Y, and then press Enter to delete all the files. When you delete all the files in a directory by using the wildcards *.* (*asterisk period asterisk*), DOS will ask you to confirm that you want to delete everything in this directory. Press Y for Yes, and the files are deleted. (Press N if you made a mistake and you don't want to delete the files.)

So Why Isn't the Directory Empty?
Even after you delete all the files in a directory, when you use the DIR command to list files, you'll see something like this:

Directory of C:\MONTHLY
```
.          <DIR>    10-16-93   3:51p
..         <DIR>    10-16-93   3:51p
    2 file(s)        0 bytes
              16957440 bytes free
```

The . (dot) represents the address of this directory, and .. (double dot) represents the address of the parent directory (which in this case is the root). Think of these dots as "bread crumbs" that DOS uses to find its way through the directory tree. These markers will not be removed until the directory itself is deleted, so don't worry about them. (You'll learn how to delete directories in Lesson 9.)

If you want to delete all the files in a directory, and the directory itself, you can do that in one step (without having to delete the files first). See Lesson 9 for details.

Restoring Deleted Files

If you delete a file accidentally, don't panic—there's a good chance you can get the file back. This is possible because DOS doesn't actually delete files. Instead of erasing the place on the disk where a file resides, DOS simply erases its *record* of the file—the file's name and location. Because DOS has no record of the file, the deleted file is essentially gone.

So how can you get it back? When DOS erases the file's name from its records, it merely changes the first letter of its name to a question mark, as in **?UDGET.DOC**. DOS knows not to pay attention to any file that begins with a question mark, so the space that the file occupies becomes available. If another file needs the disk space, it is written on top the deleted file, replacing the old data—therefore, *you must act quickly* to retrieve deleted files with any hope of success.

Back to the Future   If you delete a file accidentally, *don't do anything*! Follow the steps in this lesson to retrieve the file. If you copy files onto the same disk where you just deleted a file, you may lose your chance to retrieve your lost file—because your copied file may have overwritten the deleted file.

A Glimmer of Hope   You can greatly improve your chances of recovering deleted files by using Delete Sentry, as explained in the next section.

You restore files with the UNDELETE command. Suppose you had just typed this:

DEL APR93.WK1

when your boss asks you to do a comparison between last month's sales (April) and this month's. How do you get the file back? Easy—just use this command:

UNDELETE APR93.WK1

Bad Command? If you get the error message **Bad command or filename** while using the UNDELETE command, you need to create a path to the \DOS directory. See Lesson 4.

When you use the UNDELETE command, you might be asked to supply the first letter of the filename, as in:

?PR93.WK1

Please supply the missing letter:

Enter the missing letter (in this case, the letter A). The file should be recovered—I say *should* be, but keep in mind that this command works best if you use it right after deleting the file. Don't copy files onto your hard drive, or use any programs, until you've recovered the deleted file. In short, *if you delete a file accidentally, do nothing until you use the UNDELETE command.*

Recovering Several Files at Once

If you've deleted not one, but several files. Use this command:

UNDELETE /LIST

The **/LIST** switch displays a listing of all the recently deleted files, along with their chances of a successful recovery (see Figure 8.1).

```
H:\>undelete /list

UNDELETE - A delete protection facility
Copyright (C) 1987-1993 Central Point Software, Inc.
All rights reserved.

Directory: H:\
File Specifications: *.*

    Delete Sentry control file contains    2 deleted files.

    Deletion-tracking file not found.

    MS-DOS directory contains    2 deleted files.
    Of those,    0 files may be recovered.

Using the Delete Sentry method.

    DELFILE  BAT    65  1-27-93  4:25p  ...A  Deleted:  9-23-93  3:50p
    QD       BAT    17  1-27-93  4:56p  ...A  Deleted:  9-23-93  3:51p

H:\>
```

Delete Sentry method for   These files can be recovered.
tracking files is being used.

Figure 8.1   You can list recently deleted files.

To undelete several files, use wildcards, as in:

UNDELETE *.BAK

Increasing Your Chances of Recovering Deleted Files

Often DOS saves files by breaking them into chunks and storing them in the first available spots, all over the hard disk. If a file was stored in pieces, UNDELETE will have a harder time recovering the file unless you use Delete Tracker or Delete Sentry. When a file is deleted, DOS remembers where the starting piece of a file is located, but it may not remember where the rest of the pieces are. The delete-protection methods listed here keep track of the exact location of each piece of a file and provide the missing information to DOS if needed, thereby increasing your chances of a successful recovery.

DOS provides two methods for increasing your chances of recovering deleted files:

- **Delete Sentry**   This method provides the best protection, but it may require up to 7% of your hard disk space. When you use this method, a hidden directory called \SENTRY is created. When you delete files, they are copied to this directory before they are deleted by DOS. When you activate Undelete, they are copied back to their original directory. Files are saved in this directory until it has grown to 7% of your hard disk space—then old files are deleted to make way for new ones.

- **Delete Tracker**   This method provides better protection than simply relying on fast action on the user's part. Delete Tracker requires a minimum of disk space, so if your hard disk is almost full, it's a good option. Delete Tracker keeps track of the file's original location on disk in a file called PCTRACKR.DEL, making it easier for DOS to undelete the file.

Using Delete Sentry and Delete Tracker to Protect Files

To install Delete Sentry, place the following command in your AUTOEXEC.BAT file (for information on how to edit your AUTOEXEC.BAT, see Lesson 20):

UNDELETE /S*drive*

With the /S switch, you replace the word *drive* with an actual drive letter, such as C. Undelete will create a \SENTRY directory on the drive you indicate. For example, to install the \SENTRY directory on your C drive, use this command in your AUTOEXEC.BAT:

UNDELETE /SC

If you have limited hard drive space, you might want to use Delete Tracker. Add the following command to your AUTOEXEC.BAT:

UNDELETE /T*drive-numfiles*

With the /T switch, you replace the word *drive* with an actual drive letter, such as C. Undelete will create the file, **PCTRACKR.DEL**, on the drive you indicate. Replace the word *numfiles* with the maximum number of deleted files you want to keep track of. For example, to install the PCTRACKR.DEL file on your C drive, and track up to 350 deleted files (a good number for a 32MB hard disk), use this command in your AUTOEXEC.BAT:

UNDELETE /TC-350

In this lesson, you learned how to delete files and how to recover them. In the next lesson, you will learn how to create and remove directories.

Lesson

Managing Directories

In this lesson, you will learn how to manage your directories: how to create them, delete them, and rename them.

Changing Directories—A Review

In Lesson 2, you learned how to change from one directory to another. To change directories, you use the CD command. As a quick review, here's what you do to change to a directory called WORD:

CD\WORD

and press Enter. There is one directory that is special because it is the main directory on your PC: the *root directory*. To change to the root directory, type

CD\

and press Enter. (The backslash (\) by itself represents the root directory.) All other directories branch off from the root. Each program that you purchase creates its own directory off of the root. For example, a program might create a directory called \WORD, \123, etc. DOS itself creates a directory called \DOS.

Creating New Directories

You can add directories to organize your files and make working with your computer easier. For example, if you use a word processor, you could add a subdirectory (under your word processing directory) called DOCS or WORK to store the documents you create. If you use a spreadsheet program, you could create a similar directory called WKS or XLS. If more than one person uses your computer, create directories where each person can store their files.

To create a directory, use the **MD** (make directory) command. The syntax for the MD command is simple:

MD [*d:*]*path*

The directory you create is placed under the current directory. If you are in the root directory, the directory you create is placed under the root. If you are in a directory called \WORD, the directory you create is placed under the \WORD directory. For example, suppose you wanted to create a new directory called **PROJECTS**, just under the root directory. Type these commands:

CD\

MD PROJECTS

You can create directories in one step by adding a path to the MD command, as in:

MD C:\PROJECTS

Now suppose you wanted to place the PROJECTS directory under your WORD directory instead of under the root. Use these commands instead:

CD\WORD

MD PROJECTS

Or use this one command that includes the complete path:

MD C:\WORD\PROJECTS

Directory   Computer files are organized in directories. Directories can be thought of as "rooms" on your PC's hard disk; every program you use has its own "room." The files that make up the program are placed in its directory.

Subdirectory   If a directory is like a room, then a subdirectory is like a closet. Subdirectories can be created to further divide a directories files. For example, you can create a subdirectory called DOCS within the word processing directory for storing your documents. In this way, the word processing directory is the *parent* directory for the subdirectory DOCS.

Root Directory   The root directory is a special directory. You can think of the root directory as a "lobby," and just as rooms branch off of a lobby, directories branch off of the root. Files that are general purpose and not program specific are placed in the root directory, such as AUTOEXEC.BAT and CONFIG.SYS.

Last Name, Please   You can add up to a three-letter extension to a directory (as in WORK.93), but this is very uncommon, and may lead to confusion with filenames, which almost always have an extension.

Listing the Directories on a Disk

In Lesson 6, you learned how to list the files in a directory with the DIR command. Directories are also listed when you use the DIR command, and they are denoted with a special **<DIR>** marker.

To list the subdirectories of your current directory, and *not the files*, use this command:

DIR *.

For example, if you change to the root directory and use this command, you'll see the main directories on your hard disk. (Those directories that are just under the root directory.) This enables you to familiarize yourself easily with a new PC:

CD\

DIR *.

If you want to see a listing of *all the directories* on a disk, use the TREE command:

TREE [*d*:][*path*][/F][/A] [I MORE]

For example, to list all the directories on your C drive, type this command:

TREE C:\ I MORE

The Path to Success   The TREE command is an external command, and as such, it will require you to enter a path to your \DOS directory in order to use it. See Lesson 4 for instructions.

The I **MORE** parameter at the end of the TREE command is not required, but often necessary because it keeps the listing from scrolling off your screen before you can read it.

The TREE command comes with two optional switches, **/F** (which causes files as well as directories to be listed) and **/A** (which is used when you print out your listing):

TREE C:\ /A >PRN

When printing a listing, omit the **|MORE** parameter because the output is not going to the screen. Instead, add the *redirection symbol*.

> **Redirection Symbol** The greater-than sign (>) is used in DOS commands to redirect the normal output of a command away from the monitor to something else, such as the printer (PRN).

Deleting a Directory

In Lesson 8, you learned how to delete just the files in a directory with the DEL command. That's useful if you need to "clean out" a directory without actually removing it. If you want to remove a directory, use the DELTREE command:

DELTREE [/Y][*d:*]*path*

For example, to delete a directory called BIGCO under your WORD directory, use this command:

DELTREE C:\WORD\BIGCO

DOS will prompt you to verify that you really want to delete the directory and all of its files. Press Y to continue (press N to abort the deletion).

> **So Long, Farewell, auf Wiedersehen, Goodnight** If you delete the directory in which files were stored, you may not be able to undelete the files.

If you don't care to be prompted, use the /Y switch (which is placed in front of the name of the directory you wish to delete):

DELTREE /Y C:\WORD\BIGCO

Renaming a Directory

There may be times when you'll want to change the name of a directory. Maybe you didn't get the name right and you keep forgetting what the directory is for, or maybe the purpose of the directory has changed. You might think that you should use the REN command to rename directories, just as you use it to rename files, but if you try, you'll get an error message because DOS just doesn't understand. Instead, use the MOVE command:

MOVE [*d:*]*olddir* [*d:*]*newdir*

For example, to rename a directory called \1992 to \1993, use this command:

MOVE C:\1992 C:\1993

The Move command creates a new directory called C:\1993, and then moves the files from C:\1992. Finally, Move deletes the files in the C:\1992 directory. Using the Move command to rename a directory is quick and easy— all these things (the creating, moving, and deleting) happen in a flash.

Wrong Moves You cannot use the MOVE command to rename a directory to an already existing directory name. You can, however, use the MOVE command to move files from one directory to another. See Lesson 7.

That Darn Path!   If you see the error message **Bad command or filename**, you need to set up a DOS path so that you can use the MOVE command. See Lesson 4 for more details.

In this lesson, you learned how to create, delete, and rename directories. In the next lesson, you'll learn how to format diskettes.

Lesson

10

Formatting Diskettes

In this lesson, you will learn how to prepare diskettes for use by formatting them.

A Simple Formatting Procedure

Formatting diskettes prepares them for use, and erases all information on the diskette. You need only format a diskette once, but it won't hurt the disk to format it many times. In fact, reformatting a disk is one way to remove the existing data on it. (Deleting all the files on it is another way—see Lesson 8.)

Diskettes must be formatted to their proper density— usually either double or high. In Lesson 2, you learned that the *density* of a diskette determines the amount of information it can hold. High-density diskettes hold at least twice as much information as the same size double-density diskettes. Can't tell what type of diskettes you have? See Lesson 2 for more help.

When you insert a new disk for formatting, DOS cannot sense which density the disk should be formatted to, so (unless you specify otherwise) DOS formats the disk to the highest density it can. If you use only diskettes which match the maximum density of your diskette drive, you will not have to worry about formatting them incorrectly, but if you use low-density diskettes in a high-density drive, there's the potential for error; see "When the Diskette Doesn't Match the Drive Type," later in this lesson.

> **Dense About Density?** If you get the error
> message **Invalid media or Track 0 bad**, DOS is
> trying to tell you that either the diskette is dam-
> aged, or you're trying to format it to the wrong
> density. See "When the Diskette Doesn't Match the Drive
> Type," later in this lesson, for more help on what to do.

> **Make It Quick** If the diskette has already
> been formatted, and you simply want to erase the
> files, add the **/Q** switch, as in FORMAT A: /Q.

You format a diskette with the FORMAT command:

FORMAT *d*:

Where *d*: represents the drive letter you wish to format,
as in:

FORMAT A:

Press Enter, and you'll be prompted to insert a diskette
into the drive. Insert the diskette and press Enter again. DOS
attempts to save unformatting information (in case you want
to reverse the formatting process), then it formats the diskette. After the diskette is formatted, you can enter an
optional *volume label* of up to 11 characters (including
spaces).

> **Volume Label** A name for a disk which is
> recorded electronically on the disk itself during
> the format process. A volume label displays when
> DIR is used to list the files on the disk.

Bad Command?   If you get the error message
Bad command or filename while using the
FORMAT command, you need to create a path to
the \DOS directory. See Lesson 4.

After a diskette has been formatted, DOS displays the
amount of space available on the diskette, as shown in Figure
10.1. Press Y to format another diskette, or N to end the
formatting process.

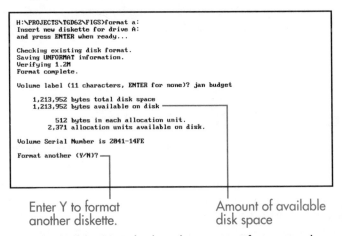

```
H:\PROJECTS\TGD62\FIGS>format a:
Insert new diskette for drive A:
and press ENTER when ready...

Checking existing disk format.
Saving UNFORMAT information.
Verifying 1.2M
Format complete.

Volume label (11 characters, ENTER for none)? jan budget

    1,213,952 bytes total disk space
    1,213,952 bytes available on disk

       512 bytes in each allocation unit.
    2,371 allocation units available on disk.

Volume Serial Number is 2041-14FE

Format another (Y/N)?
```

Enter Y to format   Amount of available
another diskette.   disk space

Figure 10.1   DOS displays the amount of space on the
formatted diskette.

Comma Copy Cat   Like the DIR command,
the DOS 6.2 FORMAT command includes
commas within its displayed information. If you
have DOS 6.0, you will not see commas.

You can format a diskette and specify a volume label
(such as *Davis Project*) at the same time with the **/V:*label***
switch:

FORMAT A: /V:Davis Project

Bad Sectors?   If *bad sectors* (unusable areas) are found on your diskette, they are marked so that DOS won't use them. You can still use a diskette with bad sectors, but don't use it for irreplaceable information, because such diskettes usually develop additional bad sectors.

Looking for Bad Spots   By default, the DOS 6.0 FORMAT command always re-evaluates each diskette during the formatting process, remarking bad sectors. The DOS 6.2 FORMAT command does not recheck already-marked bad sectors. To force it to do so, add the /C switch.

Making a Bootable Diskette

A *bootable diskette* can be used to boot your system in the case of an emergency. Prior to DOS 6, a bootable diskette was a staple. If the installation of a new program caused your system to lock up because it made unauthorized changes to your AUTOEXEC.BAT and CONFIG.SYS, you could use the bootable diskette to start your system and make repairs.

Booting   The process of starting your PC and loading the operating system (DOS) into memory.

Help Is on the Way!   With DOS 6.2, you can bypass a defective CONFIG.SYS and AUTOEXEC.BAT completely by pressing F5 at startup. Pressing F8 at startup will allow you to select which lines in the CONFIG.SYS and AUTOEXEC.BAT to bypass.

With the new startup feature, a bootable diskette may not be necessary for the same reasons it once was. However, you still need a bootable diskette in case your hard disk becomes inaccessible, or if your system contracts a virus, as explained in Lesson 17. To make a diskette bootable, add the /S switch, as in:

FORMAT A: /S

The /S parameter tells DOS to copy the system files onto the diskette, making it bootable.

When the Diskette Doesn't Match the Drive Type

If you need to format a diskette which does not match the type of drive your computer uses, you must specify the size of diskette (in bytes) with the /F:*size* switch:

FORMAT A: /F:360

If you don't use the /F switch and specify the correct size (capacity), DOS will either refuse to continue (saying the disk is bad) or will try to continue, but will find so many bad sectors that the disk's format will be unstable.

> **Just My Size**   For a double-density 5 ¼-inch diskette, type /F:360; for a double-density 3 ½-inch diskette, type /F:720.

Unformatting a Diskette

You may be able to unformat a diskette that was formatted accidentally. If you use Delete Sentry (explained in Lesson 8), your chances are even better.

To unformat a diskette:

1. Place the diskette in its drive.

2. Type UNFORMAT *drive:* where ***drive:*** is replaced by the letter of the diskette drive, as in UNFORMAT A:.

3. If you want to test the unformat procedure first, you can press the Spacebar and type /TEST, as in UNDELETE A: /TEST.

4. When prompted, type Y to proceed with the unformat.

Bad Command?   If you get the error message **Bad command or filename** while using the FORMAT command, you need to create a path to the \DOS directory. See Lesson 4.

Can You Keep a Secret?   You can protect your sensitive data by formatting a diskette *unconditionally.* Add the **/U** parameter, as in FORMAT A: /U. This reformats each sector of the disk, completely wiping away the previous contents. *Diskettes formatted in this manner can not be unformatted.*

In this lesson, you learned how to format diskettes. In the next lesson, you will learn how to perform other diskette operations.

Lesson

Other Diskette Operations

In this lesson, you will learn how to copy diskettes, and how to check disks for bad sectors without reformatting them again.

Copying Diskettes

You should always make a copy of new program diskettes to keep as a backup in case the originals get damaged in some way. You should also make a copy of your original DOS diskettes. In addition, you may want to copy your own work diskettes as backups.

The Great Switch If you're making a copy of a high-density diskette using a single drive, don't be surprised if you have to switch diskettes several times during the copy process. However, if you have DOS 6.2, DISKCOPY now uses the hard disk for buffering—so switching diskettes more than once during the copying process is a thing of the past.

Copy Cat! When copying diskettes, you must use the same size and density as the original diskette. For example, you can't copy using DISKCOPY from a 5 1/4-inch disk to a 3 1/2-inch disk.

You copy diskettes with the DISKCOPY command:

DISKCOPY *sourcedisk*: *destinationdisk*:

For example, to copy a diskette using drive A, insert the *original diskette* into the drive and type:

DISKCOPY A: A:

The first drive letter is the *source drive* (where the original disk is placed) and the second drive letter is the *target* or *destination drive* (where the target disk is placed). These are often the same drive letters, as in **A: A:**. Be sure to follow each drive letter with a colon, and separate them with a space.

After typing the DISKCOPY command, verify that the source (original) disk is in the drive, then press Enter. When prompted, remove the original diskette, and insert the destination (target) disk in the drive. (You will not have to switch diskettes if you use two different drives.) After the copying procedure is done, you can copy an additional diskette by typing Y at the prompt that asks, **Copy another diskette?**

> **Let's Go for a Drive**   You must enter two drive letters (such as A: A:) with the DISKCOPY dialog box, or you will get the error message **Invalid drive specification. Specified drive does not exist or is non-removable.** In addition, you cannot use a drive letter which indicates a hard disk, such as drive C. You can only use diskette drive letters, such as A: and B:.

> **Unrecognizable**   If you get the error message **Bad command or filename** when you enter the DISKCOPY command, you need to add a path to the \DOS directory. See Lesson 4.

You can verify the accuracy of the copying as it proceeds by adding the /V (verify) switch, as in:

DISKCOPY A: A: /V

This slows down the copying process considerably, but it catches errors before they can cause trouble.

You can also compare two diskettes after using the DISKCOPY command to verify that an exact copy has been made. Simply type:

DISKCOMP A: A:

and press Enter. (Be sure to use the same drive letters as you did with the DISKCOPY command.) Insert either the original or the copy, wait until prompted, then switch to the other diskette. If there is any difference between the two diskettes, you'll see a message indicating the sector(s) where the difference(s) were found.

> **Fast Switch**   If you are using one drive for the disk copy process, you will probably switch diskettes several times. DOS 6.2 copies information to the hard disk during the copy process, so you will only swap diskettes once. To force the DOS 6.2 DISKCOPY command to use memory only, and not the hard disk, add the **/M** switch.

Checking Disks

If you want to list the files on a disk, use the DIR command in Lesson 6. If you want to check the status of a disk and make repairs, use the command SCANDISK. Although you can use ScanDisk command on diskettes, it's much more important that you use ScanDisk periodically on your hard disk, to clean up after DOS.

Checking It Out!   If you have DOS 6.0, the
SCANDISK command is not available. Use the
CHKDSK command instead: **CHKDSK C: /F.** It
does not detect and repair all the problems that
ScanDisk does; however, it can repair lost
cluster/lost chain problems.

As you learned in Lesson 8, when you delete a file, it's
not really deleted. Instead, the reference to where that file is
located is erased, and the area is marked "available." Sometimes, DOS is not as neat as it needs to be, and an area will
be marked "used" even after the file reference is erased. This
creates a *lost cluster* or a *lost chain*. When the opposite
happens—two file references lay claim to the same area—it's
called a *cross-linked file.*

Lost Clusters and Lost Chains   Lost clusters and chains are pieces of files that have been
"lost" by DOS. When you delete a file, it is not
actually erased; instead, the reference to the file's
location is erased. If a file's location is erased
from the file listing but its address is still marked "used,"
you get a lost cluster. If several of these clusters occur
together on the disk, you get a lost chain.

To clean up these and other organizational problems,
use ScanDisk. In addition, ScanDisk can be used to perform a
surface scan (to check for physical damage) and check and
repair damage to DoubleSpace drives (see Lesson 13). To use
ScanDisk to check the status of drive C for example, *exit all
programs first.* Then use this command:

SCANDISK C:

Network News   Don't try to use SCANDISK
on a network drive, such as drive F.

Bad Command? If you get the error message
Bad command or filename when you enter the
SCANDISK command, you need to add a path to
the \DOS directory. See Lesson 4.

You can have ScanDisk verify several drives at once, by
simply specifying the drive letters:

SCANDISK C: D:

or by adding the /ALL switch:

SCANDISK /ALL

If you want ScanDisk to check for problems *but not to
fix them,* use the /**CHECKONLY** switch. To check for
problems and *repair them automatically,* use the
/**AUTOFIX** switch:

SCANDISK C: /AUTOFIX

As long as you haven't used the /**CHECKONLY** or
/**AUTOFIX** switches, ScanDisk will prompt you when it
encounters problems, and give you a choice as to how to
proceed: **F**ix It, **D**on't Fix It, or obtain **M**ore Info. To make a
choice, press the bold letter or click on the button with your
mouse. For example, to select **F**ix It, click on it or press **F**.

If your drive has lost clusters or chains, ScanDisk will
ask you if you want it to create a file to contain the data that
was in each lost cluster, as shown in Figure 11.1. The data is
probably unusable because it's part of an old file. You can
delete the file by pressing **L** or clicking on De**l**ete. If you'd
rather have ScanDisk delete them automatically as they
occur, add the /**NOSAVE** switch:

SCANDISK C: /NOSAVE

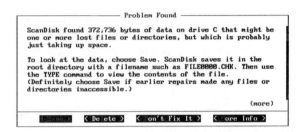

Figure 11.1 ScanDisk prompts you when it encounters problems.

At a particular point, ScanDisk will prompt you to insert a *blank* diskette which you can later use to undo the repairs if you so choose. To later undo the repairs performed by ScanDisk, insert the Undo diskette, and type this command:

SCANDISK C: /UNDO

At a later point, ScanDisk will ask you if you want it to perform a surface scan on the disk. This type of scan detects physical errors on the disk, and it should be performed periodically. To perform the scan, press Enter. To bypass it, press N for **No**. In addition, you can have ScanDisk perform a surface scan without prompting you by adding the **/SURFACE** switch.

At the end of its program, ScanDisk will allow you to view a log of its results (shown here in Figure 11.2), and to save that log if you wish. Simply click on View Log (or press V), then Save Log (or press S). The log is saved in the file SCANDISK.LOG, and it's located in the root directory of the scanned drive. If you want a detailed explanation of the problems encountered, click on More Info or press Enter. To exit ScanDisk, press X or click on Exit.

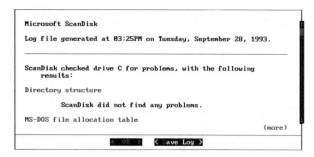

Figure 11.2 You can view a log of ScanDisk's results.

In this lesson, you learned how to copy diskettes and how to check disks for problems. In the next lesson, you will learn how to increase the storage space on your hard disk with DoubleSpace.

Lesson 12

Doubling Your Disk Space with DoubleSpace

In this lesson, you will learn how to double your hard disk space with DoubleSpace.

What Is a Compressed Drive?

Disk compression programs such as DoubleSpace can store more information on a disk because data is stored more densely than with MS-DOS alone. If you use DoubleSpace, your hard disk can increase its capacity by almost two times.

When you install DOS 6.2, your drives are still uncompressed. You must run DoubleSpace to compress a drive. After you install DoubleSpace, your hard disk will consist of two sections, as shown in Figure 12.1. One small section will remain uncompressed, to support the few programs and system files that cannot run on a compressed drive.

You can use a drive compressed with DoubleSpace the same way you would use any regular drive; the only difference is that it will store more files than it normally would. Unbelievable? The next section explains how it's done.

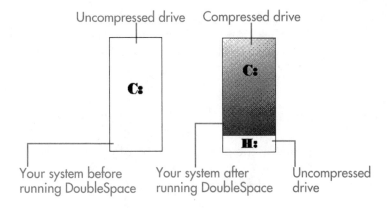

Figure 12.1   Before and after DoubleSpace installation.

Check Those Utilities   If you depend on
third-party utilities such as PC Tools and Norton
Utilities, make sure that they are compatible with
a DoubleSpace drive. If you're not sure, consult the
manual or call the manufacturer before you run these
programs.

How DoubleSpace Works

If you don't care about how DoubleSpace works (but are
simply grateful that it does), you can skip this part.

After DoubleSpace installation, your physical C: drive is
unaltered. But there is a huge file that takes up most of it
now. This huge file, called DBLSPACE.000, is your compressed drive. DOS assigns a drive letter to this file, so you
can access your files from it.

> **Logical Drive**   The DBLSPACE.000 file is not
> really a drive. DOS pretends that it is, so the files
> within it can be read normally. A drive that is not
> physically a drive is called a *logical drive*.

All the files that were formerly on your hard disk are
compressed into DBLSPACE.000, along with most of the free
space remaining on the drive. A little bit of free space is left
outside of DBLSPACE.000 (uncompressed) in case you need
it.

Here's the tricky part. DOS knows that you expect all
the files that were on C: before to be accessible from C: now.
So it assigns the drive letter C: to the *compressed* drive, and
changes the name of the *real* C: drive to something else
(usually **H:** or **I:**). That way you can still do everything from
the C: prompt, just as you did before you compressed your
hard disk.

> **For Your Protection**   The new DOS 6.2
> DoubleSpace includes DoubleGuard, which
> protects the DoubleSpace data in memory
> against accidental corruption from errant pro-
> grams. If you're using DOS 6.0 DoubleSpace, it's worth
> the cost of the upgrade to get this additional protection.

Using DoubleSpace to Compress a Drive

> **Is There No Looking Back?**   If you're
> using DOS 6.0, you cannot easily reverse the
> compression process. If you have DOS 6.2,
> however, you can now decompress a drive
> (assuming you have enough room). Use the Tools
> Uncompress command within the DoubleSpace utility.
> (See Lesson 13 for details on using the DoubleSpace
> feature.)

It takes roughly 1 minute per megabyte of data to compress your hard disk, so you might want to start the DoubleSpace Setup program at the end of the day, and run it overnight. To set up DoubleSpace, follow these steps:

> **Scanning for Signs of Life**   DOS 6.2 uses ScanDisk (see Lesson 11) to verify the integrity of a drive before it compresses it. (This reduces the risk of problems later on.) If you use DOS 6.0, you should run a disk utility such as Norton Utilities' Disk Doctor or PC Tools' DiskFix to verify your disk's integrity before running DoubleSpace.

1. Exit all programs.

2. Change to the DOS directory by typing CD\DOS and pressing Enter.

3. Start the DoubleSpace Setup program by typing **DBLSPACE** and pressing Enter.

4. Choose between Custom or Express Setup. (Unless you are an experienced user, select Express Setup.) If you'd like to run Custom Setup to compress a drive other than C or to create an empty compressed drive, press F1 to obtain more information.

5. A small section of your drive will remain uncompressed. If you want to change the default letter for the uncompressed drive, do so before pressing Enter.

6. A message will appear which tells you how long the compression process will take. This is a one-time process that takes about 1 minute per megabyte. Press C to Continue (which will complete the compression process) or Esc to exit (which will stop it).

7. After the disk compression is finished, a summary
    will display showing information on the com-
    pressed drive. Press Enter and your system will
    restart with the compressed drive active.

Here's Looking at You, Kid   Typing DIR
drive: /C (where *drive* is the drive letter) will
display information about a compressed drive.

Now that you have a compressed drive, you use it as
you would normally. Copy programs or files, create or delete
directories, or delete files as normal.

In this lesson, you learned about disk compression, and
how to use DoubleSpace to compress a disk. In the next
lesson, you'll learn how to run the DoubleSpace utility
program, and how to compress a floppy diskette.

Lesson 13

Other DoubleSpace Operations

In this lesson, you will learn how to run the DoubleSpace utility program.

Now That I Have a Compressed Drive, What Do I Do with It?

In Lesson 12, you learned how to compress your disk drive. But now that it's compressed, what do you do? Well, you work with your compressed drive as you would with any other drive. The compression process remains invisible to you, the user.

The DoubleSpace utility program allows you to perform these compression functions:

- Increase the storage capacity of diskettes by compressing them.

- Adjust the size of your compressed drive.

- Display information about the compressed drive.

- Format a compressed drive.

- Defragment a compressed drive. (You'll learn more about defragmenting a drive in Lesson 14.)

- Check a compressed drive's integrity.

You access the DoubleSpace utility program by typing
DBLSPACE at the DOS prompt.

Is There an Echo in Here?   Yes, this is the
same command you used to start compressing the
drive in the first place, but it serves a different
purpose now that the drive is already compressed.

External Command   If you see the error
message **Bad Command or Filename** when
entering the DBLSPACE command, you need a
path to the \DOS directory. See Lesson 4 for
details.

To open a menu and issue a command, simply click on
the menu to open it, and click on a command. With the
keyboard, press Alt and hold it down, then press the bold
letter in the menu you wish to open. For example, to open
the Tools menu, press Alt+T. Once a menu is open, press the
underlined letter of the command to select it.

To exit the DoubleSpace utility program, open the
Drive menu by clicking on it or pressing Alt+D. Then select
the Exit command by clicking on it or pressing X.

Compressing a Diskette

You can use DoubleSpace to increase the storage capacity of
your *high-density* diskettes (you cannot use DoubleSpace on
a double-density—360K or 720K—diskette). After a diskette
has been compressed by DoubleSpace, it becomes immediately available for copying files, etc.

Compression Depression You can only use a compressed diskette on a PC that uses DOS 6 or 6.2, and is running DoubleSpace (the PC has one or more compressed drives).

Don't Touch That Dial! If you use DOS 6.0, do not remove the double-spaced diskette or reboot your PC while you are using a compressed diskette. If you do, you will need to use the Mount command to make the diskette available again. Simply insert the diskette, start the DoubleSpace utility, open the Drive menu, and select the Mount command. If you use DOS 6.2, you don't need to worry about mounting or unmounting—compressed diskettes are recognized automatically by the system.

You can only compress a diskette if you have already run the DoubleSpace setup program (see Lesson 12). To compress a diskette:

1. Insert the diskette in its drive.

2. At the DOS prompt, type DBLSPACE and press Enter.

3. Open the Compress menu.

4. Select the Existing Drive command. The dialog box shown in Figure 13.1 is displayed.

5. Highlight the drive and press Enter.

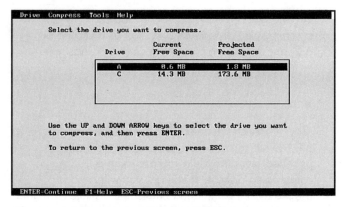

Figure 13.1   Compressing a diskette is easy.

6. Return to DOS by selecting the Exit command from the Drive menu.

7. Now that the diskette has been compressed, use the diskette as you would any other.

> **Mount Up!**   If you use DOS 6.0 and you remove a compressed diskette, you will need to remount it in order to use it again. You can mount a compressed disk quickly by typing DBLSPACE /MOUNT drive: and pressing Enter. (Substitute an actual drive letter for **drive:** in the command—as in DBLSPACE /MOUNT A:.)

Uncompressing a Drive

If you have enough room on your disk to store the uncompressed files, you can reverse the DoubleSpace process. Before you uncompress a drive, you should back up its files. See Lesson 15 for more information.

Also, it takes roughly the same amount of time to uncompress a drive as it took to compress it (approximately 1 minute per megabyte of data), so you might want to start the DoubleSpace Uncompress program at the end of the day, and run it overnight.

> **Uncompression Depression** If you use DOS 6.0, you will not be able to uncompress a drive. Reformat the drive and restore your data from a backup performed prior to the compression process.

To uncompress a drive:

1. At the DOS prompt, type DBLSPACE and press Enter.

2. Open the Tools menu.

3. Select the Uncompress command.

Follow the additional instructions on the screen. When it's done, your drive will no longer be compressed.

Displaying Compression Information

You can display information about your compressed drive, such as the amount of available space, the amount of defragmentation (see Lesson 14 for more information), and the compression ratio (the ratio of compressed disk space to formerly uncompressed space—a compression ratio of 2:1 would reflect a drive whose space had exactly *doubled* through disk compression).

To display disk compression information:

1. At the DOS prompt, type DBLSPACE and press Enter.

2. Open the Drive menu.

3. Select the Info command. The dialog box shown in Figure 13.2 is displayed.

```
┌──────── Compressed Drive Information ────────┐
│  Compressed drive H is stored on uncompressed drive C │
│  in the file C:\DBLSPACE.001.                         │
│                                                        │
│        Space used:              110.52 MB             │
│        Compression ratio:         1.7 to 1            │
│                                                        │
│        Space free:               11.82 MB             │
│        Est. compression ratio:    1.7 to 1            │
│        Fragmentation:                 7%              │
│                                                        │
│        Total space:             122.34 MB             │
│                                                        │
├────────────────────────────────────────────────────┤
│   ███ K ███  ⟨  ize ⟩  ⟨  atio ⟩  ⟨  elp ⟩         │
└────────────────────────────────────────────────────┘
```

Figure 13.2 Display information about your compressed drive with the DoubleSpace utility.

You can list the compression ratio for individual files with a variation of the DIR command:

DIR /C

When you add the /C switch, you see the compression ratio for each file, as shown in Figure 13.3.

```
H:\PROJECTS>dir /c

   Volume in drive H is COMPRESSED
   Volume Serial Number is 12FB-154F
   Directory of H:\PROJECTS

   .            <DIR>        03-29-93    4:58p
   ..           <DIR>        03-29-93    4:58p
   MYSTUFF      <DIR>        03-29-93    4:58p
   TGD62        <DIR>        09-17-93    2:01p
   OUTLINES     <DIR>        03-29-93    4:58p
   WWI          <DIR>        03-29-93    4:59p
   WED          <DIR>        04-23-93    9:35a
   ALPHABKS     <DIR>        09-20-93   10:10a
   TGDPGCNT XLS      17,364  09-21-93    1:11p   3.2 to 1.0
   COMMON   STY       3,584  08-23-93   10:20a   4.0 to 1.0
   OUTLINE  DOC       8,192  09-22-93    3:42p   2.3 to 1.0
   OWPW         <DIR>        09-02-93    8:03a
                    3.1 to 1.0 average compression ratio
          12 file(s)        29,140 bytes
                        12,378,112 bytes free

H:\PROJECTS>
```
Compression ratio for this file

Total compression ratio for the files listed

Figure 13.3 You can display file compression information with the DIR command.

In this lesson, you learned how to compress a diskette with DoubleSpace, and how to use the DoubleSpace utility. In the next lesson, you will learn how to check your disks for defragmentation problems with DEFRAG.

Defragmenting a Drive

In this lesson, you will learn how to defragment compressed and non-compressed drives.

Why Defragment a Drive?

When a file is copied onto a drive by DOS, parts of the file are often split up over different sections of the drive, in order to make the most effective use of available space. *Defragmenting* a drive causes those parts of files that were split up to be placed back together.

On an uncompressed drive, fragmentation can cause a drop in speed when accessing files. This is because when a file is *fragmented* (split up) over a drive, it takes longer to locate and read each separate part of the file. If the file is placed on the drive in contiguous pieces, the entire file can be read much more quickly.

Defragmenting a compressed drive may not affect speed as much as on an uncompressed drive, but it will usually result in additional available space on the drive. This is because a compressed drive is really just one big file, and reorganizing it does not really reduce the time needed to locate that single file on the drive.

Hurry Up and Wait   Defragmenting a
large drive may take a while, especially if it is
badly fragmented. If you have DOS 6.0, you
may want to upgrade. DOS 6.2 takes less time
to defragment a drive because it now uses extended
memory to hold the files temporarily as it reorganizes
them.

How to Defragment an Uncompressed Drive

To defragment an uncompressed drive, *exit all programs
(including Windows),* then use the DEFRAG command:

DEFRAG *d*: [/U][/S*sortorder*]

External Command   If you see the error
message **Bad Command or Filename** when
entering the DEFRAG command, you need a path
to the \DOS directory. See Lesson 4 for details.

(Remember, the stuff in square brackets is optional.)
For example, to defragment drive C, type this command:

DEFRAG C:

DEFRAG will analyze the drive and make a recommen-
dation for the best optimization method. Press Enter to begin
optimization. (Figure 14.1 shows an example of optimization.) You'll see a message telling you when the drive is
optimized. Press Enter to continue. You can then optimize
another drive, re-optimize this drive (using a different optimization method), or exit the DEFRAG utility. Use the arrow
keys to choose an option, and press Enter to select it.

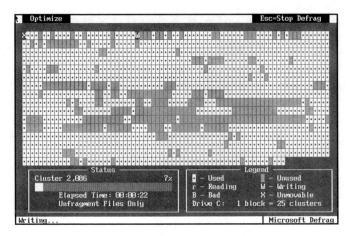

Figure 14.1 DEFRAG optimizes your drive by reorganizing files.

Controlling the Blank Spaces

By default, DEFRAG reorganizes the files on the drive so that any empty space is located at one end of the drive. This arrangement takes a bit more time to accomplish. If you wish to have DEFRAG relocate all the pieces of a file so that they are together, but you don't care if some empty spaces exist between files, use the /U option:

DEFRAG C: /U

Using the /U option will save you time in defragmenting a drive, while still affording you the speed benefits of having all the pieces of a file located in contiguous spaces on a drive. If you have a large drive, or not a lot of time, the /U switch is the way to go.

Putting Files into a Specific Order

You can also specify the order in which files are organized on the drive. Normally, files are organized in the order in which they are located. To specify a sort order for the files, use the /S switch. The sort order does not affect the physical order of the files on the drive, but how they are organized in the file allocation table (FAT), and therefore, how they are displayed when you type DIR to list files.

There are many options for the /S switch:

N or –N   Sort files by filename.

E or –E   Sort files by extension.

D or –D   Sort files by date and time of last change.

S or –S   Sort files by size.

Placing a minus sign in front of an option causes a reverse order to be used. For example, this command sorts files alphabetically by filename:

DEFRAG C: /SN

While this command sorts files in *reverse* alphabetical order by filename:

DEFRAG C: /S–N

Defragmenting a Compressed Drive

Use the DoubleSpace utility to defragment a compressed drive. (You can use the DEFRAG command at the DOS prompt to defragment a compressed drive, but there are several switches that you must specify. Therefore, it's simpler and easier to use the DoubleSpace utility, and let it specify the correct parameters for you.) Although defragmenting a compressed drive will not necessarily result in an increase in speed, it might possibly increase the available space on the compressed drive.

> **Just My Size?**   If you try to change the size of your compressed drive (making it larger or smaller), you will probably be asked by DoubleSpace to defragment the drive first. In addition, after adjusting its size, DoubleSpace will often spontaneously defragment the drive for you.

1. At the DOS prompt, type **DBLSPACE** and press Enter.

> **DOS Path**   If you see the error message **Bad Command or Filename** when entering the DBLSPACE command, you need a path to the \DOS directory. See Lesson 4 for details.

2. Select the drive you want to defragment from those listed.

3. Open the Tools menu.

4. Select the Defragment command.

5. You'll see a message asking whether you really want to do this. Click on Yes or press Enter to continue.

6. After the drive is defragmented, open the Drive menu and select Exit to return to DOS.

In this lesson, you learned how to optimize your drives by defragmenting them. In the next lesson, you'll learn how to back up your important files.

Lesson

15

Backing Up Your Hard Disk

In this lesson, you will learn how to back up your hard disk.

An Overview of Backup

What's New, Pussycat? DOS 6.0 and
6.2 come with a backup utility called *MS
Backup*, which is easier to use than the
BACKUP command from prior versions. MS
Backup is the same in both DOS 6.0 and DOS 6.2.

A *backup* is a copy of the files on your hard disk. There are
three types of backups:

Full backup This backup is a complete copy of
every file on your hard disk.

Incremental backup This backup copies only the
files that have been changed since the last full or
incremental backup. To restore a complete hard disk,
*you would need your full backup and all sets of
incremental backup diskettes*.

Differential backup This backup copies only the
files that have been changed since the last full backup.

To restore a complete hard disk, *you would need your full backup and the latest set of differential backup diskettes.*

Here's a Plan   As a good rule, perform a full backup once a month, then perform either an incremental or differential backup at the end of each work day. If you don't perform your full backups often, do an incremental backup every day, because it won't take as long as a differential backup.

Keepsakes   If you perform incremental backups, keep all of them until you perform your next full backup. If you perform differential backups, you can keep just the latest set. Never reuse your full backup diskettes for an incremental or a differential backup.

When a backup is performed, a *backup catalog* is created. A backup catalog is a file which contains information about what was backed up, and when. The backup catalog is copied to both the hard disk and the last backup diskette. The backup catalog is used when restoring files.

To perform a backup, you must select the drives, directories, and the files to be backed up. These selections can be stored permanently in a *setup file*, so you can reuse them at a later date. MS Backup comes with a few setup files already created for common situations, such as a full backup.

The first time you run MS Backup, it will configure itself. To do this, MS Backup will run some tests on your system. You will need two diskettes of the same size and density as the diskettes you will use when you do real backups. Follow the on-screen instructions, and remember to save the configuration when the tests are over.

Performing a Full Backup

To Format or Not to Format   You do not
have to have preformatted diskettes to perform a
backup; MS Backup will format diskettes as
needed. However, using already-formatted
diskettes will make the backup process go a lot faster.

Before you begin, here's how you'll make selections within
the MS Backup utility:

*   *With a mouse*, simply click on an option to select
    it.

*   *With the keyboard*, press and hold the Alt key.
    Then press the **bold letter** of the option you wish
    to select.

Now let's begin. Follow these steps to back up an entire
disk drive:

1.   Type **MSBACKUP** and press Enter.

External Command   If you see the error
message **Bad Command or Filename** when
entering the MSBACKUP command, you need a
path to the \DOS directory. See Lesson 4 for
details.

2.   Choose Backup. The Backup dialog box, shown in
Figure 15.1, appears.

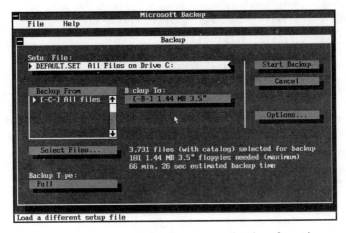

Figure 15.1   You can configure your backup from the Backup dialog box.

3. In the Backup From box, select the drive to back up. MS Backup will display **All Files** next to the drive letter you select.

4. Repeat step 3 for additional drives.

5. If you are going to use diskettes of a type or size different from the one listed, change the drive letter in the Backup To box.

6. Select Start Backup.

7. When the backup is complete, press Enter to return to DOS.

Performing an Incremental or Differential Backup

An incremental backup differs from a differential backup. *Differential* backs up any file that has been changed since the last full backup; *incremental* backs up only those files that have been changed since either a full or an incremental backup (whichever was more recent). Performing an incremental or differential backup of your entire hard disk is easy:

1. Type **MSBACKUP** and press Enter.

   A Path to Success   If you see the error message **Bad Command or Filename** when entering the MSBACKUP command, you need a path to the \DOS directory. See Lesson 4 for details.

2. Choose Backup. The Backup dialog box appears.

3. In the Backup From box, select the drive to back up. MS Backup will display **All Files** next to the drive letter you select.

4. Repeat step 3 for additional drives.

5. If you are going to use diskettes of a type or size different from the one listed, change the drive letter in the Backup To box.

6. In the Backup Type box, select Incremental or Differential.

7. Select Start Backup.

8. When the backup is complete, press Enter to return to DOS.

Backing Up Selected Directories and Files

You may want to back up only certain directories or files. Since all your program files are on the original diskettes, and they don't change, why back them up? By backing up only the directories which contain the files you create, you can reduce the time it takes to do a full backup.

Safety First   You may want one full backup of your system (complete with program files) in case of hard drive failure.

To back up selected directories or files:

1.   Type **MSBACKUP** and press Enter.

Command Path   If you see the error message **Bad Command or Filename** when entering the MSBACKUP command, you need a path to the \DOS directory. See Lesson 4 for details.

2.   Choose Backup. The Backup dialog box appears.

3.   If you are going to use diskettes of a type or size different from the one listed, change the drive letter in the Backup To box.

4.   In the Backup Type box, select Full, Incremental, or Differential.

Making a Difference   If you want to back up all the files in a selected directory, regardless of when they were last changed, select Full.

5. If necessary, in the Backup From box, select the drive whose files you want to back up.

6. Choose Select Files, and the Select Backup Files dialog box appears, as shown in Figure 15.2.

Unselected directories   Unselected files

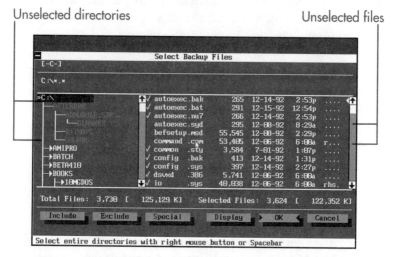

Figure 15.2 Back up selected files and directories with the Select Backup Files dialog box.

7. Select the directories or files to back up:

With the mouse Double-click (or click with the right mouse button) on a file or directory to select it. To select multiple files or directories, click the left mouse button and hold, click the right mouse button, then drag until the group is selected.

With the keyboard Use the Spacebar to select directories or files.

Make Your Selection, Please An arrow indicates selected directories. If all the files in a directory are not selected, it is displayed with a double arrow. A checkmark indicates selected files within a directory.

8. When you are done selecting files, select OK.

9. Select Start Backup.

10. When the backup is complete, press Enter to return to DOS.

You can also select files by using Include and Exclude in the Select Backup Files dialog box. Select Include or Exclude, then follow these steps:

1. Enter a directory path, such as C:\WORD\DOCS.

2. Enter a filename pattern, such as *.DOC.

3. Decide whether to include or exclude subdirectories.

4. Select OK.

Using Special in the Select Backup Files dialog box, you can exclude additional files, such as:

• Files based on the date they were last changed.

• Copy-protected files

• Read-only files

• System files

• Hidden files

In this lesson, you learned how to back up your hard disk. In the next lesson, you'll learn how to restore files to your hard disk if they get damaged.

Lesson

Restoring Your Hard Disk

In this lesson, you will learn how to restore your hard disk.

Restoring a Full Backup

If something happens to an important file you need (such as a data error or an unrecoverable deletion), you will need to restore that file from a backup. To restore a single file, see the section called "Restoring Selected Directories and Files" later in this lesson.

However, if the situation is worse (for example, a computer virus has "eaten" most of your files), you'll need to use a recent backup to perform a *complete restore* (restoration) of your system. Here's how you restore a full backup:

1. Type **MSBACKUP** and press Enter.

   > **External Command** If you see the error message **Bad Command or Filename** when entering the MSBACKUP command, you need a path to the \DOS directory. See Lesson 4 for details.

2. Choose Restore. The Restore dialog box, shown in Figure 16.1, appears.

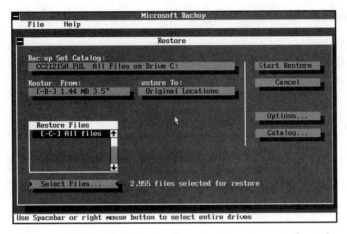

Figure 16.1 You can configure your restoration from the Restore dialog box.

3. In the Restore Files box, select the drive to restore. Use the drive that the files were backed up from, regardless of whether you want to restore the files to a different drive.

4. Press the Spacebar or click the right mouse button on the drive, and **All Files** will be displayed next to the drive letter you select.

5. Repeat step 3 for additional drives.

6. If you are going to use diskettes of a type or size different from the one listed, change the drive letter in the Restore From box.

7. If you want to restore files to different drives or directories from which they were backed up, select Restore To.

8. Select Start Restore.

9. When the restore is complete, press Enter to return to DOS.

Restoring Selected Directories and Files

Sometimes you may want to restore only certain directories
or files. For example, if you deleted an important directory
from your hard disk accidentally, you need to restore it from
your backup diskettes, rather than using the UNDELETE
command. (The UNDELETE command cannot restore files to
a deleted directory.) To restore selected directories or files:

1. Type MSBACKUP and press Enter.

> **Bad Command?**   If you see the error message
> **Bad Command or Filename** when entering the
> MSBACKUP command, you need a path to the
> \DOS directory. See Lesson 4 for details.

2. Choose Restore. The Restore dialog box appears.

3. If you are going to use diskettes of a type or size
   different from the one listed, change the drive letter
   in the Restore From box.

4. If necessary, in the Restore Files box, select the
   drive whose files you want to restore. Use the drive
   that the files were backed up from, regardless of
   whether you want to restore the files to a different
   drive.

5. Choose Select Files, and the Select Restore Files
   dialog box appears, as shown in Figure 16.2.

Selected files

```
─                        Select Restore Files
[-C-]

C:\*.*

»C:\                 ↑  autoexec.bak      265    12-14-92   2:53p  ...a  ↑
 ↳ NETWORK              autoexec.bat      266    12-14-92   2:53p  ...a  ◄
   ↳ QUICKNET.SDK       autoexec.syd      295    12-08-92   8:29a  ...a
    ↳ BLRNKER           befsetup.msd   55,545    12-08-92   2:29p  ...a
   ↳ BITMAPS         √ command .com    53,485    12-06-92   6:00a  r...
   ↳ SBROS           √ common   .sty    3,584     7-01-92   1:07p  ...a
  ↳ VIM.PRO          √ config  .bak      413    12-14-92   1:31p  ...a
  ↳ BATCH            √ config  .sys      397    12-14-92   2:27p  ...a
  ↳ META-LIB         √ dsvxd   .386    5,741    12-06-92   6:00a  ...a
  ↳ TOOLS            √ io      .sys   40,038    12-06-92   6:00a  rhs.
   ↳ TCM-DOS       ↓ √ mirorsav.fil      41    11-24-92   3:34p  rhsa ↓

Total Files: 2,959 [   84,211 K]   Selected Files: 2,955 [   84,156 K]

   version     Print      Special      Display  ►  OK  ◄   Cancel

Select entire directories with right mouse button or Spacebar
```

Figure 16.2   Restore selected files and directories with the Select Restore Files dialog box.

6.   Select the directories or files to restore:

With the mouse   Double-click (or click with the right mouse button) on a file or directory to select it. To select multiple files or directories, click the left mouse button and hold, click the right mouse button, then drag until the group is selected. To select non-contiguous files or directories, press Ctrl and click on each item.

With the keyboard   Use the Spacebar to select directories or files.

> **Make Your Selection, Please**   Selected directories are displayed with an arrow. If all the files in a directory are not selected, it is displayed with a double arrow. Selected files within it are displayed with a checkmark.

7. When you are done selecting files, select OK.

8. If you want to restore files to different drives or directories from which they were backed up, select Restore To.

9. Select Start Restore.

10. When the restore is complete, press Enter to return to DOS.

If more than one version of a file exists on your different backup sets, the most recent version is the one DOS restores. You can select a different version by using Version from the Select Restore Files dialog box.

Using Special in the Select Restore Files dialog box, you can exclude additional files from restoration:

- Files based on the date they were last changed

- Copy-protected files

- Read-only files

- System files

- Hidden files

In this lesson, you learned how to restore files if they become damaged. In the next lesson, you will learn how to keep your system safe from viruses.

Lesson 17

Keeping Your System Safe from Viruses

In this lesson, you will learn how to detect and remove computer viruses.

What Is a Computer Virus?

A *virus* is a program that infects your computer in various ways, such as changing your files, damaging your disks, and preventing your computer from starting.

You can infect your system any time you copy or download files onto your disk, or boot from a diskette. You can protect yourself from serious damage by:

- Maintaining a recent backup of your files.

- Checking diskettes for viruses before copying files from them. *Be sure to check program disks before installing new software.*

- Write-protecting program diskettes to prevent infection.

- Running VSafe, a special DOS 6 virus-detection program, all the time.

- Never starting your computer with a diskette in the drive. (Make a virus-free bootable diskette for emergency purposes—see the next section.)

- Running Microsoft Anti-Virus (another DOS 6 program) as soon as a problem occurs.

Creating a Startup Diskette

You can create a virus-safe startup diskette by following the instructions in Lesson 10. After the diskette is formatted, add the following files:

- CONFIG.SYS

- AUTOEXEC.BAT

- MSAV.EXE

- MSAV.INI

- MSAV.HLP

- MSAVIRUS.LST

- MSAVHELP.OVL

Make Room!   If your emergency diskette does not have enough room for all of these files, copy just the CONFIG.SYS and the AUTOEXEC.BAT onto the diskette. Then copy the Microsoft Anti-Virus program onto another diskette, and keep both of them together in a safe place.

Current Affair   Keep your system files current by copying your CONFIG.SYS and AUTOEXEC.BAT files onto your emergency-startup diskette whenever you modify them.

After you've copied these files onto the diskette, w*rite-protect* it to prevent infection. If you ever need the diskette, you'll have a good copy of your system files and the virus detection program.

> **Protect Your Writes!** To write-protect a
> 5 1/4-inch diskette, affix a write-protect tab to
> the notch on the right-hand side of the diskette. To
> write-protect a 3 1/2-inch diskette, slide the write-
> protect indicator downwards, so that the hole is visible.

Scanning for Viruses

If you suspect a virus, follow these steps immediately to scan your disk:

1. Exit all programs, including Windows.

2. Boot your system with your startup diskette.

3. At the DOS prompt, type **MSAV /A /C** and press Enter. (If you are connected to a network, type **MSAV /L /C**. This will limit scanning to local drives only). The /A switch indicates that all the drives should be scanned, whereas the /L switch indicates local drives only. The /C switch tells the anti-virus program to *clean* viruses off the drive if it finds them.

The Anti-Virus Main Menu appears, as shown in Figure 17.1. All local drives are scanned and cleaned of any viruses found.

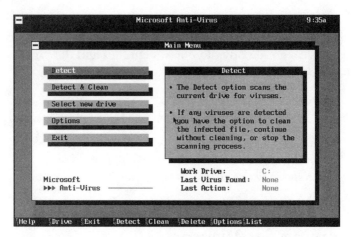

Figure 17.1 Select scanning options from the Anti-Virus screen.

Stop That Scan! You can stop the scan process at any time by pressing F3.

If any viruses are detected, a dialog box will appear, offering several options:

- Choose Update to update the checksum for a file that was changed with your knowledge (and not by a virus).

- Choose Clean to clean the virus from your system.

- Choose Continue to ignore the virus, but continue scanning. If you know that a file was changed legitimately, use this option.

- Choose Stop to stop the scanning process and go to the Anti-Virus Main Menu.

- Choose Delete to delete the infected file from your system. Use this option if the file has been destroyed by a virus, and you wish to prevent further infection.

Keeping Up with the Times   New viruses are invented every day. Keep your virus detection current by updating the list of viruses. See your DOS manual for more details.

Controlling the Virus Scan

If you prefer to control the virus scanning manually, type MSAV at the prompt. From the Anti-Virus Main Menu, select from among these options:

External Command   If you see the error message **Bad Command or Filename** when entering the MSAV command, you need a path to the \DOS directory. See Lesson 4 for details.

- If necessary, press F2 or choose Select new drive to change the drive you want to check for viruses.

- Press F8 or choose Options to change various scanning options, such as disabling the alarm sound and creating a report of the virus scan.

- Start the scan by selecting either Detect (F4) or Detect & Clean (F5). If you choose Detect, you will be able to select a course of action if an infected file is detected.

Performing Virus Scans Automatically at Startup

To perform a scan of your hard disk every time you boot your computer, add the following command string to your AUTOEXEC.BAT file (for more information on editing your AUTOEXEC.BAT file, see Lesson 20):

```
MSAV /N
IF ERRORLEVEL 86 GOTO VIRUSDETECT
ECHO Relax. No viruses were detected.
GOTO END
:VIRUSDETECT
ECHO Viruses were detected. Run MSAV /A /C.
:END
```

If you are attached to a network, use this command string instead:

```
MSAV /N /L
IF ERRORLEVEL 86 GOTO VIRUSDETECT
ECHO Relax. No viruses were detected.
GOTO END
:VIRUSDETECT
ECHO Viruses were detected. Run MSAV /L /C.
:END
```

With one of these command strings in place, your hard disk will be scanned automatically at startup, and you'll see a message telling you whether or not you need to run MSAV to clean viruses off your system.

Performing Continuous Virus Detection

Using the MSAV command at startup will only detect viruses that are active at that time. To have ongoing protection, run VSafe. VSafe is a program that runs in the background as you perform your normal computer tasks. VSafe will warn you of changes to your files that might be caused by viruses. To start VSafe automatically every time you boot your computer, add this command to your AUTOEXEC.BAT (for more information on editing your AUTOEXEC.BAT file, see Lesson 20):

VSAFE

In this lesson you learned how to detect and prevent viruses. In the next lesson, you will learn how to improve your PC's memory usage.

Lesson 18

Making the Most of Your System's Memory

In this lesson, you will learn how to optimize your system's memory.

What Is Memory?

Your computer comes with two kinds of memory: *RAM* (*random access memory*) and *ROM* (*read-only memory*). ROM stores the permanent instructions your computer needs to operate. RAM is a temporary storage area used by your programs.

When you start a program, it is loaded into RAM and it starts executing instructions. As you work on a letter or some other file, that file is kept in RAM so changes can be made. If you create large documents, your program requires large amounts of RAM to manipulate the information in the document. Your program loads other files into RAM as needed—if you spell-check your letter, for example, the spell-check program is loaded into memory where the main program can use it.

All programs need memory in order to run—some need quite a lot of memory. Not having enough memory can affect the way your programs work—and even prevent some programs from starting. It is vital that you make the most of the memory your computer has.

How Much Memory Does Your Computer Have?

Memory is divided into *bytes*. A byte stores a single character, such as the letter Q. A *kilobyte* (1KB) is roughly 1,000 bytes (it's really 1024 bytes). A *megabyte* (1MB) is roughly 1,000,000 bytes (it's really 1,048,576 bytes). RAM is divided into several areas:

Conventional memory   The first 640KB of RAM. Conventional is the most important area of memory, because it's the only part of memory in which a program can run.

Upper memory   Memory above 640KB and below 1MB. Usually this area is reserved for your system's use, but pockets of unused space (called *upper memory blocks*) can be converted for use by device drivers and memory-resident (TSRs, or terminate and stay resident) programs.

Memory-Resident Programs   Also known as *TSRs* or *terminate-and-stay-resident* programs. These are programs (like VSafe) which load into memory and "go to sleep" until something activates them.

Device Driver   A special program that controls optional devices, such as a mouse or a network card.

Extended memory   Memory above 1MB; it cannot be used to run programs, but only to store data temporarily. Only certain special programs (such as Windows, DESQview, and AutoCAD) can use this area of memory. Programs such as these access extended memory not through DOS, but through a special *extended-memory manager*, such as EMM386.EXE (which comes with DOS 5 and 6). The ability to access extended memory through an extended-memory manager must be written into an application specifically—otherwise, that program will not use extended memory, even if you load EMM386.EXE.

High memory   The first 64KB of extended memory. With the help of a high-memory manager such as HIMEM.SYS, DOS can access this area of extended memory directly. High memory is a good place to store device drivers, memory-resident programs, or even DOS itself.

Expanded memory   Special memory that is linked to DOS through a window in upper memory. As with extended memory, programs can use expanded memory only indirectly—through the use of an expanded-memory manager—and it is much slower than extended memory.

Memory Poseurs   Extended memory can sometimes be made to simulate expanded memory. You would want to do this if you had a program which needed expanded memory and not extended memory. Although expanded memory simulated in this manner would occupy the same physical space as extended memory, the method that a program uses to access that memory is quite different (via a different memory manager), so if you convert part of your system's extended memory into expanded memory, only programs which use expanded memory can access that section of RAM.

To see how much memory your system has (and of what type) enter this command:

MEM

and press Enter. A listing similar to Figure 18.1 will appear. From this listing, you can determine the amount of each kind of memory being used. (Adapter RAM/ROM is memory located on add-on boards such as video boards.)

> **Pass the Commas, Please** If you have DOS 6.0, you'll notice a subtle difference between what you see displayed on your screen, and the figure shown here. DOS 6.2 added commas to the output of the MEM command to make it more legible.

```
C:\>mem

Memory Type        Total  =   Used  +   Free
-----------------  -----     -----     -----
Conventional        640K       61K      579K
Upper                91K       68K       23K
Reserved            384K      384K        0K
Extended (XMS)*   2,981K    1,509K    1,472K
                  ------    ------    ------
Total memory      4,096K    2,022K    2,074K

Total under 1 MB    731K      129K      602K

Total Expanded (EMS)             1,408K (1,441,792 bytes)
Free Expanded (EMS)*               928K (950,272 bytes)

* EMM386 is using XMS memory to simulate EMS memory as needed.
  Free EMS memory may change as free XMS memory changes.

Largest executable program size    579K (592,448 bytes)
Largest free upper memory block     23K (23,600 bytes)
MS-DOS is resident in the high memory area.

C:\>
```

Figure 18.1 Seeing how much memory your system has.

> **External Command** If you see the error message **Bad Command or Filename** when entering the MEM command, you need a path to the \DOS directory. See Lesson 4 for details.

To display a listing of programs (shown in Figure 18.2) currently loaded into memory, use the MEM command with the /C switch:

MEM /C /P

The /P switch tells the MEM command to list only one screen's worth of information at a time. To see the next screen-full of information, press Enter.

```
Modules using memory below 1 MB:

Name        Total        =   Conventional    +   Upper Memory

MSDOS       16,813  (16K)      16,813  (16K)          0   (0K)
SETVER         864   (1K)         864   (1K)          0   (0K)
HIMEM        1,120   (1K)       1,120   (1K)          0   (0K)
EMM386       4,144   (4K)       4,144   (4K)          0   (0K)
SMARTDRU    29,984  (29K)       2,496   (2K)     27,488  (27K)
COMMAND      2,928   (3K)       2,928   (3K)          0   (0K)
SHARE        7,648   (7K)       7,648   (7K)          0   (0K)
SAVE         9,248   (9K)       9,248   (9K)          0   (0K)
MOUSE       17,296  (17K)      17,296  (17K)          0   (0K)
ANSI         4,288   (4K)           0   (0K)      4,288   (4K)
DBLSPACE    37,712  (37K)           0   (0K)     37,712  (37K)
Free       616,288 (602K)     592,640 (579K)     23,648  (23K)

Memory Summary:

Type of Memory      Total    =   Used     +   Free

Conventional      655,360        62,720      592,640
Upper              93,056        69,408       23,648
Press any key to continue . . .
```

Figure 18.2   Which programs are using memory?

Maximizing Memory with MemMaker

MemMaker is a diagnostic program that comes with DOS 6 and DOS 6.2. MemMaker is designed to optimize the way your system uses memory by changing your configuration files. In order to use MemMaker, you must have a 386 or 486 processor and extended memory.

Expecting Miracles?   MemMaker is great, but it's not perfect. You can optimize your system's memory usage beyond what MemMaker can do for you. If you want to know more about memory and how to make the most of it, read *10 Minute Guide to Memory Management*.

MemMaker is very easy to use, and it provides fairly good results. To optimize your system with MemMaker, follow these steps:

1. Type **MEMMAKER** and press Enter. A screen appears, welcoming you to MemMaker.

2. Press Enter and a message appears, asking you to choose between **Express Setup** (the easiest) and **Custom Setup** (for confident users) optimization. To use Express, press Enter. To switch to Custom, press the Spacebar, then Enter. The Express option works well for most systems. If you are an advanced user with a good understanding of memory management, you can use Custom optimization to free up a bit more memory. If you use Custom optimization and need additional help, press F1 at any time.

Bad Command? If you see the error message **Bad Command or Filename** when entering the MEMMAKER command, you need a path to the \DOS directory. See Lesson 4 for details.

3. A message appears, asking you if you use any programs that require expanded memory. Press Y for Yes, or N for No. Press Enter to continue.

Expanding Your Horizons If you are not sure whether your programs need expanded memory or not, check their manuals. If a program requires expanded memory, it will be clearly marked. If you're in doubt, answer N for No. If a program won't start and it says it needs expanded memory, then rerun MemMaker and answer Y for Yes.

4. Press Enter, and MemMaker will reboot your computer and verify your current configuration.

5. MemMaker makes changes to your AUTOEXEC.BAT and CONFIG.SYS (your old files are saved with a .UMB extension). Press Enter, and MemMaker will test your new configuration.

> **MemMaker Blues?** If your system locks up (freezes) while MemMaker is testing, you can reboot your system and MemMaker will pick up where it left off. To reboot, press Ctrl, Alt, and Delete at the same time.

6. Wait until a message appears, asking whether your new configuration is OK. Press Y for Yes or N for No. Press Enter to continue.

7. If there is a problem, MemMaker can undo its changes, or allow you to do further testing. Press Enter to undo changes (MemMaker will ask you to confirm), or press the Spacebar and then Enter to keep the changes.

8. A listing showing your system's memory usage appears. Press Enter to exit MemMaker.

> **Memories . . .** To undo the changes made by MemMaker at any time, type MEMMAKER /UNDO and press Enter.

In this lesson, you learned how to maximize your memory with MemMaker. In the next lesson, you'll learn how to edit a file with the DOS editor, EDIT.

Lesson

Editing a File with the DOS Editor

In this lesson, you will learn how to edit text files such as CONFIG.SYS and AUTOEXEC.BAT using the DOS editor.

A Word Before You Edit

When you edit your configuration files, keep these things in mind:

- Do not edit CONFIG.SYS or AUTOEXEC.BAT without a startup diskette handy. Instructions for making a startup diskette are covered in Lesson 10 and Lesson 18.

- If you make changes to a configuration file, make sure you reboot your PC to make those changes effective.

> **Copy Cat!** It is a good practice to make a copy of your original file before you start editing. Follow the procedures outlined in Lesson 7 to copy current versions of your CONFIG.SYS and AUTOEXEC.BAT files onto your boot diskette.

Using the DOS 6 Editor

An easy-to-use, full-screen text editor called EDIT (the DOS Editor) comes with DOS 6 and DOS 6.2. Although it is beyond the scope of this book to teach you everything you might need to know about using EDIT, this lesson will teach you enough to edit simple files such as CONFIG.SYS and AUTOEXEC.BAT.

Getting Down to BASICs   The DOS Editor is a QBASIC-driven program. QBASIC is installed in the DOS directory during installation. Do not delete the QBASIC files, or the DOS Editor will not work.

Starting the DOS 6 Editor

Follow these steps to start the DOS 6 Editor:

1.   Change to the directory which holds the file you want to edit. (To edit CONFIG.SYS or AUTOEXEC.BAT, change to the root directory by typing **CD** and pressing Enter.)

2.   Type **EDIT** and press the Spacebar.

External Command   If you see the error message **Bad Command or Filename** when entering the EDIT command, you need a path to the \DOS directory. See Lesson 4 for details.

3.   Type the name of the file you want to edit, and press Enter to execute the command. The file you requested is opened, as Figure 19.1 shows.

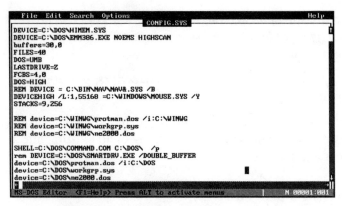

Figure 19.1   The CONFIG.SYS file is ready to edit.

Making Changes

Once a file is open, you can make changes to it. Although there are many ways to move around the screen, the methods used most commonly are those shown in Table 19.1.

Table 19.1   Moving around the DOS Editor.

To move:	Press:
Up, down, left, or right	Arrow keys
To the beginning of a line	Home key
To the end of a line	End key
To the beginning of the next line	Ctrl+Enter
To the top of the window	Ctrl+Q, then E
To the bottom of the window	Ctrl+Q, then X

When you start the DOS Editor, you are in *Insert mode*. That means when you position your cursor and start to type, what you type is inserted at that point. If you want to type over existing characters, press the Insert key. You are now in *Overtype mode*. Change back to Insert mode by pressing Insert again.

If you want to delete some characters, position your cursor on any character, and use the Delete key.

To insert a blank line before the line the cursor is on, position your cursor at the beginning of an existing line and press Enter.

Saving Your File

After making changes to your file, you must save it before exiting the Editor. To save your changes:

1. Open the File menu.

2. Select the Save command.

3. If you want to keep your original file intact (without changes) and save this file under a new name, press A from the File menu or click on the Save As command. Type the new filename and press Enter.

Exiting the DOS Editor

After you have saved your changes, you can safely exit the Editor.

1. Open the File menu.

2. Select the Exit command. You will be returned to the DOS prompt.

Made a Mistake? If you decide, after making changes to a file, that you do not want to save those changes, simply exit the Editor without saving.

Lesson 20

Configuring Your System

In this lesson, you will learn how to configure your system through the CONFIG.SYS and AUTOEXEC.BAT files.

What Is the **AUTOEXEC.BAT?**

The AUTOEXEC.BAT is a special file that *automatically executes* commands when you boot (start) your PC. By placing commands in the AUTOEXEC.BAT, you can make changes to the DOS environment or start programs. The AUTOEXEC.BAT is placed in the root directory of your boot drive, which is usually drive C.

> **Monkey See**   To view your AUTOEXEC.BAT file, type this command:
>
> **TYPE C:\AUTOEXEC.BAT**
>
> and press Enter.
>
> To view your CONFIG.SYS file (discussed in the next section) type this command:
>
> **TYPE C:\CONFIG.SYS**
>
> and press Enter.

Monkey Do   To add any of the commands in this lesson to your AUTOEXEC.BAT or your CONFIG.SYS, use the DOS Editor. See Lesson 19 for help.

Here are some of the typical commands in an AUTOEXEC.BAT:

- **PATH**   Provides DOS with a list of directories to search for program files not located in the current directory. As you may recall from Lesson 4, you need a PATH statement like this in order to access the external DOS commands:

  PATH=C:\DOS

  You can add additional directories to the search path by separating them with a semicolon (;):

  PATH=C:\DOS;C:\WINDOWS;C:\NU

- **SMARTDRV.EXE**   This command, placed in the AUTOEXEC.BAT by the DOS setup program, creates a *RAM cache*:

  C:\DOS\SMARTDRV.EXE

RAM Cache   An area of RAM which is used for storing copies of the files requested most often. Files in RAM are quicker to access than files on disk. Program performance improves when often-requested files are kept in RAM.

- **PROMPT**   Customizes the DOS prompt (see Lesson 3). This is one of the most popular variations of the PROMPT command:

  PROMPT PG

- **TSRs**   Special utility programs which load into RAM and then "go to sleep" until they are "awakened" by some event or keypress. The virus-detection program, VSAFE, is a TSR.

What Is the CONFIG.SYS?

The CONFIG.SYS file is used to customize DOS. The CONFIG.SYS can change system parameters or load special *device drivers*. Like the AUTOEXEC.BAT, the CONFIG.SYS is placed in the root directory of your boot drive, which is usually drive C.

Device Drivers   Special programs which interpret commands for optional devices, such as a mouse, network card, tape-backup, or CD-ROM drive. Device drivers can also be used to configure memory (RAM) for special purposes.

When you *boot* (start) your PC, DOS checks for the presence of a CONFIG.SYS file. The specified device drivers are loaded into RAM, and system parameters are changed as requested. If no CONFIG.SYS file exists, the default values for the system parameters are used.

Effective Immediately?   When you make changes to your CONFIG.SYS file, you must reboot your PC in order for those changes to take effect.

Here are some of the typical CONFIG.SYS commands:

- **Device Drivers**   As explained earlier, device drivers provide an interface between DOS and some piece of equipment, such as a mouse. Device drivers can also be used to configure memory. Here are some typical device drivers that are often loaded at start-up, and their purpose:

   DEVICE=C:\DOS\MOUSE   Used to configure a mouse.

   DEVICE=C:\DOS\HIMEM.SYS   Used to access upper memory, typically with the idea of moving the DOS operating system out of conventional memory. See Lesson 18.

   DEVICE=C:\DOS\EMM386.EXE   Used to access extended memory, or to create expanded memory from extended. See Lesson 18.

   DEVICE=C:\DOS\ANSI.SYS   Used to access the extended DOS character set.

- **DEVICEHIGH**   A variation of the DEVICE command which loads the device driver into upper memory, as in this command:

   DEVICEHIGH=C:\DOS\DBLSPACE.SYS /MOVE

- **BUFFERS**   Disk buffers increase the speed of your PC by storing recently requested information, in a manner similar to a RAM cache. Programs typically specify the number of buffers they require for peak performance. A database program may require 20 to 30 buffers, while a word processor may only need 10 to 15. Use a number that provides the best performance for all of your programs.

A typical BUFFERS statement looks like this:

BUFFERS=10

- **FILES**   Tracks open files. Like BUFFERS, most programs specify the maximum number of files they need to track at any one time. A typical FILES statement looks like this:

FILES=30

- **FCBS**   FCBS stands for **File Control Block System**, an area of RAM which tracks open files in a manner different from the FILES command. Most programs do not require the FCBS statement, which usually looks like this:

FCBS=4,0

- **STACKS**   Tracks the number of *interrupts*. Interrupts are sent by the PC's various hardware components (keyboard, mouse, disk drives, etc.) to get the CPU's attention. For example, when you press a key or click a mouse button, an interrupt is created— that is, an interrupt is sent to tell the CPU to stop what its doing and pay attention. A typical STACKS statement looks like this:

STACKS=9,256

> **Interrupts**   A means for a hardware component (such as the keyboard) to get the attention of the CPU.

- **SHELL**   Specifies where the DOS command interpreter, COMMAND.COM, is located. A typical SHELL statement looks like this:

SHELL=C:\DOS\COMMAND.COM C:\DOS /P

Interrupting System Startup

When your PC boots, DOS checks for the CONFIG.SYS file and executes the commands in it. Once the system environment has been defined, DOS looks for the AUTOEXEC.BAT file and executes the commands in it.

You can interrupt the processing of either the CONFIG.SYS or the AUTOEXEC.BAT by pressing F5 at startup after the beep. For example, if you're having problems with your system, you may want to bypass the command that loads a memory driver or starts Windows.

No Double Trouble If you need to, you can bypass the mounting of your double-spaced drive by pressing Ctrl+F5 after the beep. However, you will not be able to access files on the double-spaced drive until it is properly mounted.

If you wish to bypass some commands but not others, press F8 instead. You'll be prompted to bypass or execute each command. If at some point you wish to simply execute the remaining commands, press Esc. To bypass the remaining commands instead, press F5.

Let's Interact *Interactive start* (F8) is not the same in DOS 6.0. Although you can select individual commands for processing within the CONFIG.SYS, you will not be able to do that with the AUTOEXEC.BAT. Instead, you can press F5 to completely bypass the AUTOEXEC.BAT.

In addition, you cannot bypass the mounting of a double-spaced drive (as described in the previous tip) with DOS 6.0.

Lesson

Defining Multiple System Configurations

In this lesson, you will learn how to define multiple system configurations which can be selected at startup.

Defining Multiple Configurations

You can define multiple configurations within your CONFIG.SYS, and select from those configurations at startup. For example, if more than one person uses the same PC, you may want to create unique configurations for each person.

Even if you are the only user, you may need a customized configuration too. For example, if you occasionally use a DOS program which requires expanded memory (such as Lotus 1-2-3 for DOS) and you use Windows (which uses extended memory), you're wasting memory some of the time. On days where you want to use your DOS-based expanded memory program, start your PC with the necessary expanded memory, and then make the remaining memory extended, for Windows to use. On days where you don't use that program, give all memory to Windows.

To define multiple configurations, start by creating a menu from which you will choose the configuration you want at startup. To create a menu, use the **MENUITEM** command:

MENUITEM=*menuname[,description]*

For example, to create a startup menu with the choices Lotus and Windows, add these three starting commands to your CONFIG.SYS:

[MENU]

MENUITEM=LOTUS, Lotus 1-2-3 for DOS Configuration

MENUITEM=WINDOWS, Windows Only Configuration

The **[MENU]** command is simply a *descriptor* which defines a block of commands within the CONFIG.SYS. You'll define two additional blocks of commands in your CONFIG.SYS file, each block beginning with a descriptor in square brackets (such as [LOTUS] or [WINDOWS]). Beneath each descriptor, you'll list the CONFIG.SYS lines that should be executed if you choose the indicated option from the menu.

[LOTUS]

DEVICE=C:\DOS\HIMEM.SYS

DOS=HIGH,UMB

DEVICE=C:\DOS\EMM386.EXE RAM 2048

FILES=20

BUFFERS=30

C:\DOS\DBLSPACE.SYS /MORE

[WINDOWS]

DEVICE=C:\DOS\HIMEM.SYS

DOS=HIGH,UMB

DEVICE=C:\DOS\EMM386.EXE NOEMS

FILES=40

BUFFERS=10

C:\DOS\DBLSPACE.SYS /MORE

It's Not My Default!   You can designate a default menu choice with the **MENUDEFAULT** command. Simply add a line such as this to your CONFIG.SYS:

MENUDEFAULT=WINDOWS,20

The first parameter, **WINDOWS**, identifies which menu block is the default. The second parameter, **20**, is optional and it defines the number of seconds to wait for the user to select a different item before the default is chosen automatically.

With the previous commands inserted into your CONFIG.SYS, the following will display when you start your computer:

MS-DOS 6.2 Startup Menu

1. Lotus 1-2-3 for DOS Configuration

2. Windows Only Configuration

Enter a choice:

Repeating Common Commands

In our sample, many commands are the same, regardless of whether you start with the Lotus or the Windows configuration. Rather than repeat the same commands throughout a CONFIG.SYS with multiple configurations, simply add a common block of commands, like this:

[COMMON]

DEVICE=C:\DOS\HIMEM.SYS

DOS=HIGH,UMB

C:\DOS\DBLSPACE.SYS /MORE

Once the common block of commands is in place and working *remove* these commands from the [LOTUS] and [WINDOWS] blocks.

If your menu choices build on each other, use the INCLUDE statement:

INCLUDE=*menuname*

For example:

[MENU]

MENUITEM=NORMAL,Normal Configuration

MENUITEM=NETWORK,Network Configuration

[NORMAL]

DEVICE=C:\DOS\HIMEM.SYS

DOS=HIGH,UMB

[NETWORK]

INCLUDE=NORMAL

DEVICEHIGH=C:\NET\NETWORK.SYS

Defining a Submenu

Sometimes you may want to give the user more than one choice. For example, there may be more than one network onto which you can log; when you decide to start up with a network configuration, you'll need to choose which network to belong to:

[MENU]

MENUITEM=NORMAL, Normal Non-network Configuration

SUBMENU=NET, Network Configurations

[NORMAL]

Your normal CONFIG.SYS startup commands would be inserted here.

[NET]

MENUITEM=SALES, Sales Network

MENUITEM=ADMIN, Administration Network

[SALES]

You would place whatever commands are needed to start up and log onto the Sales network here.

[ADMIN]

You would place different network startup commands here—to log you onto the Admin network if you select this menu item instead.

Defining Alternate Configurations for Your AUTOEXEC.BAT

You can have DOS execute different commands in your AUTOEXEC.BAT that are based on the menu item chosen when the CONFIG.SYS is executed. Just repeat the descriptors before the block of AUTOEXEC.BAT commands to be executed, but precede them with colons rather than putting them in square brackets. For example:

PROMPT PG

C:\DOS\SMARTDRV.EXE

GOTO %CONFIG%

:SALES

PATH=C:\DOS;C:\NET

NET LOGON SALES1

GOTO END

:ADMIN

PATH=C:\DOS;C:\NET;C:\WORD;C:\ADMIN

NET LOGON ADMIN1

:END

The PROMPT and the SMARTDRV commands at the beginning of the AUTOEXEC.BAT are executed regardless of what the user chooses from the CONFIG.SYS menu. However, only one of two different paths and log-on commands will be issued, depending on the CONFIG.SYS menu option chosen by the user.

In this lesson, you learned how to create multiple configurations for your CONFIG.SYS and your AUTOEXEC.BAT. This is the last lesson. For your convenience, Appendix A provides instructions for entering commands through the DOS Shell. Appendix B provides a handy reference to the DOS commands covered in this book. Appendix C provides a summary of what's new in DOS 6.2.

Appendix

Using the DOS Shell

The DOS Shell is a graphical interface that makes it easier to issue common DOS commands, such as COPY, MOVE, and DEL. You can even start multiple programs from the Shell, and switch between them.

What, No Shell? The DOS Shell is only available with DOS versions 6.0, 5.0, and 4.0. If you upgrade to DOS 6.2, you still have the Shell program. If you purchased a computer with DOS 6.2 already installed and you wish to use the Shell, you can request a copy of the Shell program from Microsoft Technical Support.

The DOS Shell Environment

You can start the DOS Shell by typing:

DOSSHELL

The **Tree** menu is used to expand and contract subdirectories. For example, in Figure A.1, the DOS directory is expanded, showing the subdirectory **DOSHELP**. A minus (–) indicates a directory which is displaying its subdirectories, and a plus (+) indicates a directory which is hiding them. Use the plus and the minus keys to expand and contract a directory.

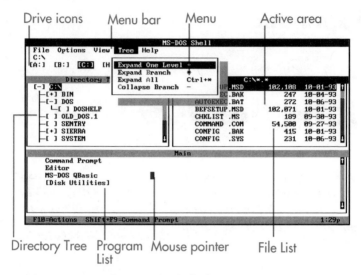

Figure A.1   The DOS 6 Shell.

À La Mode

When you start the DOS Shell, it starts in *text mode* (a display mode that uses lines and such to show screen elements). If your PC has a monitor that supports graphics, you can change the DOS Shell display to *graphics mode* (a display mode that uses pictures and boxes to show screen elements), as shown in Figure A.2.

You can also select from several screen resolutions, which determine the number of text lines that fix on your screen at once. The higher the resolution you select, the smaller (and harder to read!) the text on your screen will appear. To change the DOS Shell to a different video mode, follow these steps:

1. Open the Options menu. (Click on it, or press Alt+O.)

2. Select the Display command. (Click on it, or press D.)

3. Choose the mode you want. Either click on it or use the arrow keys to highlight it.

4. Click on OK or press Enter. The screen changes to the resolution you selected.

Drive icons   Expanded directory   File List

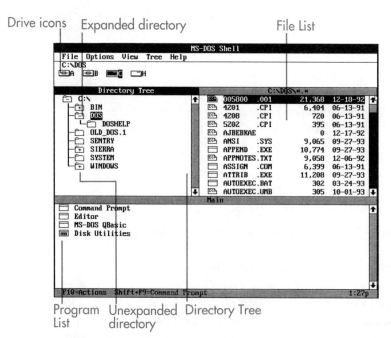

Program   Unexpanded   Directory Tree
List   directory

Figure A.2 Here's what the Shell looks like in graphics mode.

Using the Mouse

The easiest way to use the Shell is with a mouse. To use the
mouse, you either *click* or *double-click* with the left mouse
button. Some actions require that you *drag* the mouse.

Click   To click with the mouse, press the mouse
button once.

Double-click   To double-click with the mouse,
press the mouse button twice in rapid succession.

Drag   To drag the mouse, first move the mouse
to the starting position. Now click and hold the
mouse button. Move the mouse to the ending
position, and then release the mouse button.

Issuing Commands

One of the best things about the DOS Shell is that you don't
type commands; instead, you just select something off a
menu, such as the one shown in Figure A.1. The Shell *menu
bar* contains five choices: **File**, **Options**, **View**, **Tree**, and
Help. To open a menu, just click on the menu name with
your mouse. Once the menu is open, you can select a command by clicking on the command name with your mouse.

Moving Between the Areas
on the Screen

To work in an area of the Shell, you must move the cursor to
that area. Moving the cursor to an area activates the area.

The Shell screen is divided into several areas:

- **The Drive Icons area**, where you choose which drive to show.

- **The Directory Tree**, which shows the directories on the chosen drive.

- **The File List**, which shows the files in the chosen directory.

- **The Program List**, which lists programs set up to run from the DOS Shell.

The active area shows up highlighted on-screen. Looking back at Figure A.2, you can see that the **Directory Tree** area is active because its title bar is darker than the title bars of the other areas. To move from one area to another in the Shell, just click with the mouse anywhere within the area you want to be in.

Changing Drives and Directories

The active disk drive is highlighted at the top of the screen. To display files on a different drive, click on that drive in the Drive Icons area.

The directory you select in the Directory Tree determines which files will show up in the File List area. To choose a different directory from the Directory Tree area, just click on a directory with your mouse. If you see a plus sign in front of a directory, that means that there are some subdirectories hiding. You can make them show their faces by clicking on the plus sign with your mouse.

Creating New Directories

You can create a new directory anywhere—under the root directory or under an existing directory:

1. Click on the Directory Tree area, and highlight the root directory (or the existing directory under which the new directory should appear).

2. Click on the File menu to open it.

3. Click on the Create Directory command.

4. Type the name of the new directory (up to eight characters), and click on OK.

Working with Files

The whole point of the DOS Shell is to work with files more easily. The following sections describe the most common file tasks you may want to perform.

Selecting Files to Work With

Before you can do something to a file (for instance, copy it or delete it), you need to select it. You can select one file or lots of files; whatever you want to work on. To select a single file, click on it. To select several files, hold down the Ctrl key while you click on the files, one by one, with your mouse. Then release the Ctrl key.

Copying Files

When you copy files, the original file is left where it is, and a copy is placed where you indicate. For example, you might want to copy files to a different directory or disk as a backup.

To copy files with the mouse, select them, and then hold down the Ctrl key. Drag the copies where you want them. (You can drag them to a drive icon in the Drive Icons area, or to a directory on the Directory Tree.) When the confirmation box appears, click on the Yes button.

Watch Those Moves Don't forget to hold down the Ctrl key when copying files with the mouse, or you may end up *moving* them instead!

Moving Files

When you move files, the files are relocated to where you indicate. For example, you might want to move files that you seldom use into a different directory to get them out of your way.

To move files with the mouse, select them, hold the Alt key down, then drag the files to their new location. You can drag them to either a different drive in the Drive Icons area, or to a directory on the Directory Tree. When the confirmation box appears, click on the Yes button.

Deleting Files (or Directories)

When a file or a directory is no longer useful, you can delete it. To delete files, select them and press the Delete or Del key. If you selected more than one file, click on OK or press Enter. To confirm the deletion of each file, click on the Yes button; to skip a file, click on the No button.

Unlike DOS, the Shell requires you to delete all the files in a directory before you can delete it. After all the files are gone and the directory is empty, highlight it on the Directory Tree and press Del. Click the Yes button when you're asked for confirmation.

Renaming Files (or Directories)

To rename a file or directory, select it, then open the File menu and choose the Rename command. Type the new name in the box that appears, then press Enter or select OK. A filename/directory name can consist of eight characters, followed by a period and an optional three-character extension.

Running Programs

You can select a program to run using several methods, but the easiest way is by using the *Program List* (located at the bottom of the screen). Within the Program List, double-click on the program's name to start the program.

If you want to run a program that's not listed on the Program List, double-click on the program file in the File List (for example, double-click on WORD.EXE to run Microsoft Word).

You can also add programs to the list by following these steps:

1. Open the File menu and select New.

2. Select Program Item.

3. Enter the program title.

4. Enter the command to start the program.

5. Enter the program directory.

6. If you want, select a shortcut key combination (consisting of Ctrl, Alt, or Shift plus a letter) and/or a password.

7. Select OK.

Exiting the DOS Shell

To exit the DOS Shell and return to the DOS prompt (C>), press F3. If you have a mouse, open the File menu and select the Exit command.

Appendix

DOS Command Reference

This appendix lists the DOS commands used most often, describes them briefly, and shows you how to type them in. For more information about a particular command, type HELP command at the DOS prompt.

CD (CHDIR)

Displays or changes the active directory.

CD\\[*path*]

Example: CD\\WORD

CLS

Clears your screen.

CLS

COPY

Copies files to a directory or disk.

COPY [*d:*][*path*][*source.ext*] [*d:*][*path*]
[*destination.ext*] [/Y]

Switch:

/Y Do not prompt before overlaying existing files.

Example: **COPY C:\AUTOEXEC.BAT A:**

DBLSPACE

Accesses the DoubleSpace maintenance program which can be used to compress a drive or a diskette, change the size of a compressed drive, or display information.

DBLSPACE

DEFRAG

Optimizes a disk by reorganizing its files.

DEFRAG *d:* [/U] [/S:*order*]

Switches:

/U	Leave empty spaces between files.
/S:*order*	Resort your drive in the following order:
N	Filename
E	Extension
D	Date
S	Size
–	Reverse sort order

Example: DEFRAG D: /S:-D

DEL

Deletes files.

> **DEL [*d:*][*path*]*filename.ext* [/P]**

Switches:

> **/P** Asks for confirmation before deleting a file.

Example: DEL *.* /P

DELTREE

Deletes a directory and its subdirectories.

> **DELTREE [/Y][*d:*] *path***

Switches:

> **/Y** Deletes the directory tree without first prompting you to confirm.

Example: DELTREE C:\WORD\JUNK

DIR

Lists files in the specified directory.

> **DIR [*d:*][*path*][*filename.ext*] [/P][/W]**

> **[/A:*attributes*][/O:*sortorder*] [/S][/B][/L][/C][/CH]**

Switches:

/P   Lists files one screen at time.
/W   Lists files across the screen.
/A   Lists files with selected attributes.
/O   Lists files in the selected order.
/S   Lists files in subdirectories too.
/B   Lists files with no heading.
/L   Lists files in lowercase.
/C   Displays disk compression information, using a default 8K cluster size.
/CH   Displays disk compression information, using the cluster size of the host computer.

Example: DIR /P

DISKCOPY

Copies a diskette.

DISKCOPY *sourcedisk*: *destinationdisk*:

Example: DISKCOPY A: A:

EDIT

Starts the DOS Editor and (optionally) loads a file to edit.

EDIT [*d:*][*path*][*filename.ext*]

Example: EDIT C:\AUTOEXEC.BAT

FORMAT

Prepares a diskette for use.

FORMAT *d*: [/S][F:*size*][/Q][/U][/V:*label*][/B][/C]

Switches:

/S Creates a bootable diskette.
/F Formats to the specified *size*.
/Q Performs a quick format.
/U Performs an unconditional format.
/V Adds a volume *label* to the formatted disk.
/B Allocates space for system files, but does not copy them.
/C Tests all sectors to see if they are usable.

Example: FORMAT A: /F:360

HELP

Accesses the DOS Help system.

HELP [*command*]

Example: HELP DISKCOPY

MD (MKDIR)

Creates a directory.

**MD [*d:*]*path*

Example: MD C:\WORD\DOCS

MEM

Displays available memory.

MEM [/P][/C][/F]

Switches:

/P Displays one screenful at a time.
/C Displays the programs in memory.
/F Lists free memory.

MEMMAKER

Runs MemMaker, a program which automatically configures your system for best memory usage.

MEMMAKER

MOVE

Moves files to the location you specify. Also used to rename directories.

**MOVE [*d*:][*oldpath*]*filename.ext*
[*d*:][*newpath*][*filename.ext*][/Y]**

MOVE *olddirname* *newdirname*

Switch:

/Y Overlay existing files without prompting.

Examples: **MOVE C:\OLDSUB C:\NEWSUB or
MOVE C:\MKTG\JFSALES.DOC
D:\SALES\DSSALES.DOC**

MSAV

Runs Microsoft Anti-Virus, which checks the indicated drives for existing viruses, and optionally removes them.

MSAV [*d*:] [/C] [/A] [/L] [/N]

Switches:

/C Removes any viruses it finds.

/A Scans all drives but A: and B:

/L Scans only local drives, not network drives.

/N Scans for viruses while not displaying the normal interface. Use this switch at startup.

MSBACKUP

Starts MS Backup, which you can use to back up or restore your hard disk or selected directories or files.

MSBACKUP

PROMPT

Customizes the DOS prompt.

PROMPT [$P][$G][$D][$T][*text*]

Options:

$P Displays current directory path.

$G Displays the greater-than sign.

$D Displays the current date.

$T Displays the current time.

text Displays the indicated text.

Example: **PROMPT $P Enter your command here$G**

RD (RMDIR)

Removes a directory if it's empty of files.

> **RD** [*d:*]*path*

Example: **RD \PROGRAMS\JUNK**

REN (RENAME)

Renames a file.

> **REN** [*d:*][*path*]*originalname.ext*
> [*d:*][*path*]*newname.ext*

Example: **REN OLDFILE.DOC NEWFILE.DOC**

SCANDISK

Locates and repairs disk problems. Can optionally undo its own repairs.

> **SCANDISK** *d:* **[/ALL][/CHECKONLY][/AUTOFIX]**
> **[/NOSAVE][/SURFACE]**
>
> **SCANDISK /UNDO** *d:*

Switches:

/ALL	Scans all disks.
/CHECKONLY	Checks for, but does not repair problems.
/AUTOFIX	Repairs problems without prompting.
/NOSAVE	Deletes, but does not save cross linked files.

| /SURFACE | Performs a surface scan. |
| /UNDO | Undoes the repairs made by a recent ScanDisk. |

TYPE

Displays the contents of a file.

TYPE [*d*:][*path*] *filename.ext* [I MORE]

Options:

| I MORE | Using the MORE filter with the TYPE command will cause the output to display one screen at a time. |

Example: TYPE C:\AUTOEXEC.BAT I MORE

UNDELETE

Restores deleted files. Also used to establish a delete file tracking system.

**UNDELETE [*d*:][*path*][/LIST][/DT][/DS][/DOS]
[/ALL][/PURGE][/LOAD][/UNLOAD][/STATUS]
[/S[*drive*]][/T[*drive*]]**

Switches:

/LIST	Lists all files that can be undeleted.
/DT	Uses the tracking file when undeleting.
/DS	Uses the delete sentry file when undeleting.
/DOS	Uses DOS when undeleting.
/ALL	Undeletes without prompting.

/PURGE	Purges the DELETE SENTRY directory.
/LOAD	Loads UNDELETE.
/UNLOAD	Unloads UNDELETE.
/STATUS	Displays status on UNDELETE.
/S	Enables delete sentry.
/T	Enables delete tracking.

Example: UNDELETE \PROGRAMS\JUNK /LIST

UNFORMAT

Unformats a diskette.

UNFORMAT *d*: [/P][/L][/TEST]

Switches:

/P	Sends output to printer.
/L	Lists files and directories found on disk.
/TEST	Verifies that an UNFORMAT can be done, but doesn't do it.

VER

Displays the current DOS version.

VER

VSAFE

Loads a memory-resident anti-virus program which detects viruses as you work.

VSAFE

Appendix

What's New in DOS 6.0 and 6.2?

This appendix briefly describes the new features and enhancements in DOS 6.0 and DOS 6.2. See the appropriate lessons for more details.

DOS 6.0 Enhancements

If you are upgrading from a previous version of DOS, such as DOS 4 or DOS 5, here is a list of enhancements that were introduced with DOS 6.0. At the end of this appendix, you'll find the additional enhancements introduced with DOS 6.2.

AUTOEXEC.BAT and CONFIG.SYS

You can define several configuration files and select which one to boot with. You can bypass commands selectively in AUTOEXEC.BAT or CONFIG.SYS, or even boot your computer without them. See Lesson 20.

DELTREE

Use the DELTREE command to delete a directory and its subdirectories, without having to remove its files. See Lesson 9 for more details.

DoubleSpace

Allows you to compress a disk or diskette so that it will hold up to two times more data. Once DoubleSpace is installed, it works invisibly. See Lessons 12 and 13 for more details.

EMM386

Improvements allow EMM386.EXE to take better advantage of unused areas in upper memory. Programs are able to use either expanded or extended memory as needed, without changing your PC's configuration.

Help

On-line Help has been expanded to a complete, graphical, on-line reference to all commands. See Lesson 5 for more details.

Interlink

Provides the ability to link two computers (such as a laptop and a desktop computer) together to transfer files, etc.

MemMaker

MemMaker configures your 386, 486, or higher PC automatically to take best advantage of the memory you have. MemMaker moves device drivers, memory-resident programs, and even DOS out of conventional memory (this feature requires extended memory), providing more working memory for all your programs. See Lesson 18 for more details.

MEM

MEM provides more details about your system's memory usage. Using the /P switch causes MEM to display information one screen at a time. See Lesson 18 for more details.

Microsoft Anti-Virus

DOS now comes with a complete and easy-to-use program for virus detection and removal, based on Central Point's Anti-Virus. There is also an Anti-Virus for Windows. See Lesson 17 for more details.

Microsoft Defragmenter

Based on the Norton Utilities, the Defragmenter can reorganize the files on your PC to allow for faster disk access. See Lesson 14.

Microsoft Mail

Provides ability to send and receive electronic mail (E-mail).

MOVE

Move files and rename directories with this versatile command. See Lessons 7 and 9 for more information.

MSBACKUP

Replacing DOS's antiquated BACKUP program is MSBACKUP, a graphical backup and restore program based on Norton Backup. See Lesson 15 for more details. A version of MSBACKUP is also provided for Windows.

POWER

Makes better use of your laptop's power.

SmartDrive

Improvements in writing and reading information allow SmartDrive to make best use of system resources.

UNDELETE

Provides better tracking and easier recovery of deleted files. There is now an UNDELETE for Windows. See Lesson 8 for more details.

Workgroup Connection

Provides the ability to use shared directories and printers.

New DOS 6.2 Enhancements

If you are upgrading from a previous version of DOS, such as DOS 4, or DOS 5, you may want to review the list of enhancements that were introduced with DOS 6.0. You'll find that list at the beginning of this appendix. In this section is a listing of the additional enhancements introduced with DOS 6.2.

DoubleGuard

Verifies data being written from memory to a DoubleSpace drive, protecting against data corruption caused by errant programs. See Lesson 12.

DoubleSpace Enhancements

Besides DoubleGuard, DoubleSpace now performs a surface scan on each disk before double-spacing it. This ensures the integrity of the compressed data. You can now uncompress a compressed drive, if you wish. In addition, compressed diskettes are now mounted automatically. See Lessons 12 and 13.

SmartDrive Enhancements

SmartDrive performs primarily read-caching. Write-caching is turned off by default. Caching of CD-ROMs is now supported.

ScanDisk

ScanDisk replaces the old command, CHKDSK, scanning disks and performing repairs. ScanDisk works on double-spaced drives, in addition to non-compressed drives.

ScanDisk repairs more damage than the old CHKDSK command. For example, cross-linked files can be accurately detected and repaired. In addition, ScanDisk can perform surface testing on a disk. See Lesson 11.

Multiple Configurations in **AUTOEXEC.BAT**

Similar to the multiple configuration enhancement for
CONFIG.SYS that was released in DOS 6.0, DOS 6.2 now
supports the same thing in the AUTOEXEC.BAT.

In addition, you can now select individual commands to
be executed at startup in both the CONFIG.SYS and
AUTOEXEC.BAT by pressing F8 when you see **Starting MS-
DOS**. See Lessons 20 and 21.

Other Enhancements

DOS 6.2 introduces many subtle but nice enhancements,
such as:

- **Faster DISKCOPY**   DISKCOPY now uses the hard
  disk to store data temporarily, which speeds the
  copy process and reduces disk swapping.

- **Copy protection**   COPY, MOVE, and XCOPY now
  prompt the user before copying a file over an
  existing version.

- **A comment on commas**   Commands which
  typically display large numbers, such as DIR, FOR-
  MAT, and MEM, now display those numbers with
  commas, as in 1,023,476.

- **Goodbye, Shell!**   The DOS Shell is not included
  with DOS 6.2, but if you're upgrading from a
  previous version of DOS, it still exists.

Index

U-V

T

W-Z